Random Stairs

Matthew Tait

Matthew Tait has somehow outdone himself yet again with Random Stairs. *The setting is evocative in its gothic flamboyance, and the characters are dark and fascinating in their own different ways. In fact, Oaklyn Castle is a setting and a character rolled into one. Once more, Tait does what he does best, grasping the reader by the wrist and taking them on an adventure both within and without – across the border between the physical world and the cosmic unknown. Climb these random stairs with Matthew Tait, but don't expect to ever come back down again!*
– Cameron Trost, owner of Black Beacon Books

DARK
CRIB
PUBLICATIONS

TABLE OF CONTENTS

ALSO BY MATTHEW TAIT

Novels
Dark Meridian
Olearia
Slander Hall
Davey Ribbon
Providence Place
Schizoid
Deception Pass

Non-Fiction
Different Masks: A Decade In the Dark

Collections
Ghosts In A Desert World

1

Gothic, bordering on medieval, Oaklyn Castle was glimpsed through the passenger window of the limousine like something goliath, its black outline evocative of a sleeping creature with spines.

While Jaison had observed the mansion before – his first expose in glossy magazines like *People* – there was an undeniable frisson of awe watching Oaklyn's turrets and windows bleed into three dimensions. Gravel crunching under tires, the limousine swerved along a serpentine driveway with an almond-shaped border.

In the center of the almond: a circus arrangement of sculpted bushes, their outline suggestive of animals. Other shrubs were pointed and obelisk, solid assertions almost …

'A little phallic, aren't they?' said the driver of the limousine. 'Do you know what Mr. Palmer said to me on the first day I came through Oaklyn's gates? He said the gardener likes to put Viagra in the roots. Quite the joker, at times, Mr. Palmer.'

Jaison said nothing, his attention once more returned to the house. Pillars (four of them) supported an overarching gabled roof. On the front elevation alone, he counted twelve windows and three separate balconies.

'It's strange …' Jaison murmured.

The driver cast a lopsided view at his passenger. 'Strange?'

'I almost never hear Boyd Palmer referred to as *Mr.* Palmer. For a second there I didn't know who you were talking about.'

A small chuckle from the driver.

'That is how one refers to their boss, yes? *Your* boss now, from what I've heard. Although I understand what you mean. When you're outside his circle, you're only aware of Boyd Palmer as a perfect smile, almost an institution.'

'Speaking of … I've heard that Boyd – *Mr.* Palmer – is not presently in residence.' *And seldom is*, he did not add.

'Unless I'm summoned to drive him somewhere – there's three of us, by the way – the whereabouts of our boss is usually above my paygrade. However, on this occasion I think you're right. Currently, the man of the manor is absent. Somewhere in Budapest, if I'm not mistaken.'

'Working on a film?'

'I suspect so. That is, after all, what movie stars do. Although … not his wife, I see.'

As the limousine braked, its driver pointed a bony finger at something beyond the windshield.

A tall woman, elegantly dressed, poised and expectant by the iron doors of the entrance.

Despite anticipating this rendezvous and knowing it was imminent, Jaison's heart began to hammer.

Even before his escort spoke, he could feel wry amusement from the man.

'Relax. I know, easier said than done, right? You're about to meet Hollywood royalty.'

At the mention of *Hollywood*, Jaison felt his mouth go numb.

'Take it from me, you've nothing to worry about.'

'I don't?'

'Mrs. Jaqus is a wonderful boss *and* person. As lovely as the world makes her out to be, really.'

Arabella Jaqus, Jaison thought wonderingly, the name itself almost mythic sounding. *Here to greet me in the flesh.*

'I've popped the trunk,' said the driver. 'Do you want me to –'

'It's one suitcase,' he replied absently, eyes still on the standing woman. 'I can manage from here.'

'I believe you can. Oh, but before you go …'

With one foot already on the asphalt, Jaison looked back at his driver, an eyebrow raised. For some obscure reason, the middle-aged man sporting an old-fashioned flat cap had never divulged his name.

'Are you English, perhaps? Welsh?'

'You detect an accent?'

'It's subtle, but there.'

'Not English. Australian.'

At this the chauffeur beamed, some personal puzzle sliding into place. 'You're an Aussie?'

'Not anymore. Though I was born there and spent most of my youth there. To be honest, I thought the accent had vanished.'

'Faint, like I said. But still evident. Good luck with everything, Mr. Winters … including your book.'

Watching the limousine putter away, Jaison wondered how much the driver knew; what specifics Arabella or her husband might have divulged concerning the ageing wordsmith who was on the cusp of being a full-time resident of Oaklyn Castle.

He knows about the novel – which probably means he knows everything.

Suitcase in hand, feeling his heartbeat begin to move again, Jaison made his way toward the tall woman waiting by the iron doors.

A luminous celebrity; a goddess in human form.

***

Once formalities were underway, Jaison felt his anxiety receding. He'd known minor celebrities – his past work, no doubt, responsible for this summons – yet Arabella Jaqus was a different order of luminary: both starlet and philanthropist whose family profile leaned more toward royalty.

Ironically, it was *not* having to shake hands that also put Jaison at ease.

With the convention largely absconded (thanks to an ongoing pandemic), a door to conversation was open.

A mischievous smile highlighting perfect teeth, Arabella said, 'Do we need to bump elbows instead? Seems to be the norm. At least, I've seen politicians doing it.'

'No bump required. I'm curious, though. How do politicians behave when the cameras are off? I imagine social distancing is something they do for show.'

Jaison, knowing full well this woman frequently broke bread with politicians, felt he could make a casual joke at their expense.

'You imagine right,' Arabella replied, her voice as mellifluous as it was on screen. 'Behind closed doors the masks come off, literally *and* figuratively. Though I suppose … people probably say the same thing about movie stars.'

I wouldn't know, he thought to answer – but held his tongue. While he didn't know his host yet, Jaison imagined ass-kissing wouldn't score him any points.

Dressed in a khaki blazer and white tee – the kind of ensemble worn to a speaking engagement – Arabella Jaqus still managed to elicit a down-to-earth persona.

Nodding at his suitcase, she said, 'Should we do this inside, Mr. Winters? I know what you're thinking.'

This surprised him. 'You do?'

'You're wondering if the interior of Oaklyn Castle is as spooky looking on the inside. It's what everybody thinks when they first arrive.'

Jaison, who realized he *had* been wondering this (at least subconsciously), picked up his suitcase and smiled.

No doubt it was a half-witted smile – the kind of silly expression reserved for someone starstruck.

Aided by the lady of the manor, iron doors featuring elaborate tile work were pried apart, their hinges producing a gothic grouse.

***

Stepping inside, Jaison was greeted with marble floors and decorative ceiling panels. What immediately sprung to mind was a Moorish influence: wide spaces augmented with interior columns; paintwork spattered with patterns decidedly Spanish.

In addition to the opulent architecture was a scent, unmistakably domestic and somewhat at odds with the surrounds.

The smell of a well-to-do family crowded with children.

As if catching wind of this thought, Arabella said, 'The whole tribe should be close. Most of them, anyway. Because I told them you were coming. The twins are holed up somewhere, doing homework. And Selena is either in the library or out on the golf course. I'll get Declan, their caregiver, to bring them around as soon as he can.'

Five paces ahead, his hostess stopped when they reached a main living area. Though no doors gave leeway, two statues with ancient Greek characteristics stood guard. Beyond them, Jaison spied a room the size of a small airplane hangar, its floor crowded with furniture and Turkish rugs. Further away, roughly half the distance to a bifurcated staircase, a large fireplace occupied the western wall like a dark and yawning mouth.

Jaison said, 'It's cliché to say … and I know you've heard it all before, but this house is truly magnificent.'

Waving a hand at their immediate surrounds, Arabella said, 'This? It's nothing, believe me. Wait until you see the rest. Wait 'til you see the *library*. Over the years, more than a few writers have called this place home, the manor itself serving as inspiration to the best of them. May I call you Jaison?'

'Of course. May I ask how large it is?'

'Overall? The entire property sits on a hundred forty-acre plot, the largest residential development on Long Island.'

'That would mean …'

'The seventh largest in the whole country,' Arabella finished, beaming. 'At last count, there were one hundred twenty rooms. Personally, I've stepped into probably half of them.'

'Did I read somewhere that Miley Cyrus used Oaklyn to shoot one of her music videos?'

Visibly delighted that Jaison possessed this knowledge, Arabella giggled. 'She *did* use this house for one of her songs. On the day, four white horses were shipped in. Neither Boyd nor I were here, but from all reports, havoc ensued. Those horses … were trotting around right where you're standing.'

Picturing stallions wandering around the furniture – and perhaps defecating on carpets – Jaison grinned. Of course, roaming horses wouldn't be the most eccentric thing to take place within these ancient walls.

There was history here that predated Arabella's famous family of natural and adopted children.

Over one hundred years of it, to be precise.

Music videos, while serving as a humorous side note, could not compare to some of the more sinister happenings during the previous century. Vaguely, he recalled a time when parts of Oaklyn were used as an orphanage. During the last great war, he'd read soldiers' barracks occupied some of the guest houses …

Arabella noticed his woolgathering. 'You're feeling somewhat overwhelmed?'

'A little,' Jaison admitted. 'Though probably not for the reason you're thinking of.'

'It's not the environment … it's that you're here at all?'

He made a sound that was half cough, half laugh. 'I'm that easy to read?'

'You don't *have* to be. Anyone in your shoes would be feeling the same thing. Overcome, that is. A week ago, you were living a normal life in a different state. Living alone and on the verge of early retirement … but you haven't published a novel for years.'

This, coming from someone he'd just met, made Jaison feel uneasy.

They've done their homework on you. Of course, they have. Arabella and her private lackeys. Did you think they would invite you into their private world on a whim?

Leaving no stone unturned, Arabella Jaqus would know more about Jaison Winters than Jaison knew himself.

'And here you are now, sharing space with a famous woman who, by virtue of marrying an equally famous man, became an exploitable commodity by the gossip media and its empire.'

Jaison said, 'When my agent called – I hadn't heard from him in months – I thought it was some sort of practical joke. Or the man was high. Right up until your driver picked me up from the airport, I *still* thought it might be a prank. A hidden camera thing, maybe.'

Arabella's smile (Jaison noticed she had a whole catalog of them), wavered between amused and devilish. Clearly, a part of her was enjoying this exchange, his groping apprehension.

No doubt she is. How many other women possessed the power to summon anyone they wished at the drop of a hat?

She said, 'I've read them all, you know.'

'Excuse me?'

'Your books. I've read them all. Even your fiction. Of course, it's your biographies and the way you approach your subjects that stand out. Your book on the Australian band *Solid State* proved to be a bestseller for you?'

'It did,' Jaison acknowledged. 'My *only* bestseller. But that can be attributed to the success of the band.'

'No, you ingratiated yourself well into their lives. Those boys in the band, who are notoriously private, opened up to you in a unique way.'

Since arriving, numerous aspects filled Jaison with awe: Oaklyn's architecture; the physical presence of Arabella herself. However, it was *this* declaration (she was a fan) that trumped everything.

The revelation, unexpected, gave rise to an image.

Arabella Jaqus, her knees drawn up in a chair, reading one of his paperback novels by the wick of candle flame.

Arabella Jaqus, contemplating the fate of characters he'd dreamt up while drunk.

The reason she sought you out is simple. Your other books have led her to believe you can pen the story of her life in an accurate manner.

From reputation, Jaison Winters was a fly-on-the-wall writer, one presently appointed to bear witness to a notorious family.

Not solely bear witness, either. I'm here like a scientist among primates, documenting their story for posterity.

Whether Arabella had come across his novels by chance or as someone genuinely interested in biopics was a mystery.

On the cusp of making this verbal, they were interrupted by a sound issuing from the top of the bifurcated staircase: the slap of soles on marble.

Heralding the arrival of two others, both children.

A boy and girl of identical age sporting outfits of matching material.

Twins, Jaison knew.

Born of Arabella Jaqus and Boyd Palmer almost eight years ago, their arrival had been foreshadowed by the kind of public scrutiny only messianic figures were usually granted. At that time, Jaison hadn't paid much attention to their dual birth. He did recall (somewhat vividly) the furor following their delivery; the millions of dollars offered up by the news media to the mother and father.

For just a *single* picture of the fraternal babes being coddled in a hospital environment.

From the summit of the marble stairs, Kingston and Vanita Palmer stared down at the newcomer in their midst.

Arabella's joy at seeing them appeared unalloyed.

'Children,' she called out. 'Come down here and meet our new guest. This is Mr. Winters. As you know, he's going to be staying with us for the foreseeable future.'

Between the children, a knowing exchange took place … something Jaison was able to observe even from a considerable distance. It was, he knew, the kind of wordless parlance germane to twins everywhere.

Proceeding in tandem together down the left staircase, Kingston asked, 'He's the new writer, isn't he, Mommy?'

A general enquiry from an innocent mind – yet it raised a whole hotbed of questions.

New writer.

Which presented the likelihood Jasion was standing in another chronicler's wake.

Vanita, a fair-haired child with the piercing green eyes of her mother, navigated the final steps. With something in her cupped hands, she came forward to greet Jaison.

'It's a charm,' she explained, and offered up

her gift in the process. 'An evil eye charm, actually. But don't let the name frighten you.'

Tentatively, Jaison held out his open hand (all the while casting a hesitant eye at the girl's mother) and accepted the proffered keepsake.

She said, 'In Turkey, that's a country, they call them Nazar Boncuk, pronounced *bon-jook*. The charm is made from blue glass and can protect you from most things in this house.'

'It's quite pretty,' he said, and meant it. 'On my holidays I've seen similar charms; however, I have to ask … you say there are things in this house I need protection from?'

Jaison's rejoinder had humorous intent, but Vanita nodded vigorously.

'It's haunted, of course. Almost all old houses are. But this one is filled with some very special ghosts.'

'*Vanita*,' came the voice of her brother, who had retreated to stand close to his mother. 'You don't need to put a scare into our guest on his first night.'

'I'm not *trying* to, Kingston. I'm just letting Mr. Winters know there are all kinds of spirits living here. And our daddy is one of them.'

Jaison raised an eyebrow. 'He is?'

'Well, he's never here. In my eyes, that makes him a ghost.'

From the stairs, more footsteps … Jaison looked up to see a middle-aged man.

Bespectacled, he wore a green cardigan. His smile, open-mouthed, was joyful and expectant. Hands stuffed into pockets; he trotted down.

Flawlessly timed, his arrival put to bed Vanita's awkward comment.

Extending his hand, the man said, 'I'm Declan Avery. My official title is caregiver. I look after the twins.'

Without thinking Jaison went to shake … then checked himself.

Which seemed to amuse the caregiver.

'I should have mentioned,' said Arabella. 'Everybody in Oaklyn is vaccinated, including the staff. Regardless, in recent months we've put real-world precautions to rest. Oaklyn is, shall we say, a world unto itself.'

This tidbit made Declan laugh.

'Isn't *that* the truth,' he said. 'Seven years I've been here, Mr. Winters, and I'm still discovering new rooms and unexplored places. In some ways, I feel like we're like one of those isolated tribes in the Amazon rainforest.'

Jaison said, 'You can call me by my first name. And that goes for everyone else.'

'Delighted to meet you, Jaison. What does a caregiver do, you ask, besides having to live with a puzzling title? Basically, I tutor these fine little humans here … and make sure their general needs are met on a day-to-day basis.'

'The children are home schooled?'

Such a question – ousted so brazenly – might ordinarily have put him at odds with an employer. Yet Jaison was relieved to see Arabella completely unmoved by it.

Because that's what I'm here for. My job is to peel back the layers of this family and discover their inner workings.

'For children living in Hollywood,' said Arabella. 'It's a common practice. Although, thank God, we're far from *that* quagmire. The pandemic has made it even more preferable.'

'I agree,' Jaison said. 'Almost everyone in my circle is now working from home.'

'But our reasons aren't geography or even the pandemic. Home education has many benefits … and it's something that Kingston and Vanita both prefer. Montha and Selena – they are a different matter. Both have chosen to study abroad at different times. Soon, Phuoc will be returning to Vietnam to complete his high school diploma.'

For the first time, Arabella was giving lip service to her three adopted children – all of whom were born in exotic corners of the world. The woman was, Jaison knew, a pioneer when it came to the Hollywood trend of adopting children with a darker skin tone; those broods who might otherwise live out their lives in poverty without the intervention of a white savior. At the time this was news, Jaison recalled being cynical of such a process – remembered his internal rationale.

Procuring an African or Asian child like they were a trophy was akin to parading them around like a fashion statement.

And yet … this type of internal monologue was typical during his boozing years.

A time when being cynical of everything and everyone was a way of life.

Lest any of this show on his face, Jaison asked, 'Will I be meeting the others today?'

'You'll meet the other children soon,' Arabella said, then giggled. '*If* we can find them. Montha will often disappear for long stretches of time. Nobody knows where.'

'I told you,' said Kingston. 'He's outside. It's where he can work on his *special* projects without …'

'Fear of judgment,' Vanita finished, smiling and looking pleased.

Declan, seemingly uncomfortable with the subject, decided to change it.

'Arabella has decreed me as both your concierge and porter on this first night. If you hand me your bag, Jaison, I can show you to your rooms.'

'Rooms?'

The caregiver winked. 'You heard right. Certain rooms in Oaklyn are more like … like a presidential suite, I suppose. And you've been assigned one.'

Jaison's grin, like something a man half his age might wear, was noted by everyone present.

***

With Declan leading, Jaison traversed the kind of hallways one might glimpse in a dream.

Pointing the way above were light fixtures resembling Japanese lanterns. Beneath Jaison's feet, the same checkered marble was evident from his time spent in the foyer. In addition to casement windows every fifteen meters or so, framed artwork lined the walls.

Initially anticipating portraits of the resident family, he was surprised to see canvas images depicting Oaklyn Castle at various stages throughout history.

A sepia-stained montage of weddings and banquets, outdoor swimming events, and soldiers.

He froze, stopping to peruse a painting of the mansion during her formative abandoned years, an artist's impression of disrepair and its accompanying chaos. In the picture, furniture detritus filled up an entire swimming pool, great mounds of it piled with the wild abandon of a waiting pyre.

The adjacent picture featured a blown-up photograph, an entire ballroom besieged with what appeared to be …

'Mannequins,' Declan said from beside him. 'Dressed to the nines, too. Look closely, you can see them sitting on barstools.'

'This is an authentic photograph? But why would –'

'Someone fill up the ballroom with mannequins? His name was Hedley, I believe. Owen Hedley. Owned Oaklyn during a period in the Fifties and let it go almost to ruin. He was, I'm told, crazier than a sack of wild weasels. And everybody around him knew it. With no family or visitors, he eventually filled up this house with dummies imported from New York. Basically, they stood in for real people.'

It was surreal to imagine … and more fantastical to see up close. Dozens of mannequins – men wearing bowler hats and women in sequined dresses – were positioned amongst filth-encrusted tables in postures of rigor mortis.

Some, he noted, held smoking cigarettes.

Others had a full beverage placed on coasters below.

'Who took the original picture?'

'That's a good question … because they were taken afterward.'

'After what?'

'Owen Hedley died not long after he created this artificial world. Drowned in his own vomit, I was told. One of his lawyers took hundreds of pictures in the aftermath. Apparently, the dummies were everywhere: the gardens, the wine cellar, even on the roof.'

Jaison mumbled an expletive.

With little doubt, a previous owner filling the mansion with mannequins was only the tip of a much broader iceberg. For all he knew, something of import might have occurred where he and the caregiver stood right now.

Domestic disagreements, fornication.

Perhaps even murder.

In every corner and niche of Oaklyn lurked a myriad of past histories …

And the ghosts who resided inside them.

'Have people published books about the house?'

Declan appeared surprised at the question. 'Of course. There must be a dozen, at least. Official and unofficial alike. But Jaison … I wouldn't be getting any ideas.'

'What do you mean?'

'You're a *writer*. And, from what I'm told, a good one. You're here to write about Arabella and her extended family … not delve into the history of Oaklyn.'

'But surely that's a part of it?'

'A small part, I suppose. Remember though, Boyd and Arabella moved into this house after the twins were born. To provide a safer environment for them away from the trappings of Tinseltown. And their strategy worked, more or less. Vanita and Kingston have made *my* job better than I ever thought it could be.'

'And what about their adopted children? How are they finding the environment?'

Once more Jaison waited for a grimace … or simply a weird look at his forthright question. But the caregiver didn't flinch.

'As Arabella mentioned, it's different with them – certainly more challenging. Not only were they whisked away to a new country and culture, they became something like celebrities overnight. Montha – whom you'll meet – has found his new life particularly demanding. Things are much improved, but there was a time when the boy acted out.'

Jaison could recall vague snapshots of the teenager: a paparazzi lightshow at some film premiere or other. In the pictures, the boy appeared forlorn, almost surly – his Asiatic features outwardly insulted by the attentions of a Western world he seemed resistant to.

Selena and Phuoc, also teenagers, appeared more reconciled to their circumstances.

Although from a picture alone, there's no way of telling.

Still studying the photograph, Jaison felt a hand on his shoulder.

'Come on,' Declan said. 'You'll have more than enough time to gawk at these in the weeks ahead. Let's get you unpacked and settled.'

***

A royal air pervaded Jaison's guest room.

Sumptuous throws and plump pillows adorned a four-poster bed.

Monochromatic paintwork accented brass fittings, skirting boards, and window rails. By the bed, an antique rotary phone was just one of many trinkets. Reflected in mirrors and standing on shelves, Jaison spied small sculptures and butterfly-shaped lamps.

Fresh flowers ornamented a circular dining table surrounded by statesmen chairs.

Depositing his one suitcase by the bed, Declan asked, 'So what do you think of all this?'

Jaison whistled. 'I think it has the feeling of a boutique I visited once in France.'

'That's a positive, I take it?'

'It's a positive.'

'Good. Arabella will be pleased. She wants her resident writer to be comfortable.'

'How could I not be? This makes my bachelor pad look like a shanty.'

'I'm afraid it's not equipped with an official writing desk … and Arabella mentioned you're someone who writes longhand. I had the idea that if we just moved the main table up to a window, you'll not only have a decent view but more than enough room to do what you do.'

Jaison eyed the table. 'Sounds perfect. Will you help me?'

After removing the flowers and placing them bedside, Declan and Jaison hoisted the table, positioning it inches from the glass after some maneuvering. Before returning for a chair, Jaison stood for a moment to appreciate the view.

A vista containing a manicured lawn.

Leading to a picturesque pond, a path cut through the middle.

Jaison said, 'In all the pictures I've seen of Oaklyn, I've never seen *that*.'

'The pond? I can't imagine you would have. It's entirely manmade. Although it doesn't look it, does it?'

Observing lichen and moss growing around a stone barrier, Jaison said, 'Not remotely. Did Boyd and Arabella have it installed?'

'They did. And until your arrival, it's been off limits to outsiders. Vanita calls it Groom Lake and has sort of claimed it as her own. Amelia takes good care of it for her.'

'Amelia?'

'She's Oaklyn's main gardener and landscaper. At the rear of the house is an old building, what used to be a chapel. Amelia lives there most weekdays but has a place of her own near Montauk Point.'

Jaison whistled again. While it was true

Arabella was the silver-screen darling, there was no denying the cinematic nature of his personal circumstances. Being summoned to this mansion itself, of course (a house reputed to be haunted), and the varied cast of characters existing inside, each with their own function and reasons for being here.

Including himself.

The resident writer.

Declan said, 'I've been told Arabella will tour the grounds with you tomorrow, among other things. Do you prefer to eat breakfast alone? If not, I can fetch you around 8 o'clock and bring you down to the kitchen to meet some of the others.'

An opportunity to see other parts of the house?

'I'll be up early,' Jaison said. 'Dressed and ready.'

For a while, Declan seemed on the precipice of saying more.

Something ominous, perhaps – something that clearly concerned him.

Instead, he simply wished Jaison luck.

Then (with a promise of returning in the morning) exited to the hallway.

Leaving Jaison Winters alone in Oaklyn for the first time.

***

His first instinct – to explore the attached bathroom or perhaps try out the bed – was superseded by an urge to establish a work station. There was his laptop, a tool whose core function served to access the Internet; however, the crux of

Jaison's writing aids were simply sharpened pencils, sheaves of white paper, and his phone for dictation.

After retrieving them from his suitcase, both paper and pencils went into a uniform arrangement on the table; a visual aesthetic in keeping with his study at home.

In the process of plugging in his laptop, Jaison heard a tentative knock on the door.

Thinking the caregiver had returned, he called out to enter.

Preceding the visitor: a scent of juniper berries, an unmistakable perfumed aroma.

Arabella.

Walking in, she said, 'I know it's late, but I was wondering if we could talk.'

Until now, Jaison's general anxiety had been curbed. Thanks (in part) to his driver's kind words and Arabella's relaxed demeanor.

Now he felt it resurfacing.

Alone again (and away from her children), perhaps the Lady of the Manor would discard her sanguine exterior and adopt a deportment more befitting someone in charge.

I could use a drink, he thought grimly, the litany as familiar as his own reflection. *A shot to take away the edge.*

Taking his silence as acquiescence, Arabella moved toward the table. Clearly approving of his work setup, she said, 'I love it. In the modern era, there aren't many writers left who prefer longhand. One of my legal aids … he told me you write up to five pages a day?'

'That's true. Though it depends on the project. And five pages longhand will often equate to about two on the laptop. It's a sluggish process, but I find the method ultimately pays off.'

Legal aids. She's referring to her attorneys. Perhaps an army of them. Lawyers who have gone through my background and work history with a fine-toothed comb.

Standing a short distance away, Jaison was able to reflect upon Arabella in a way previously denied him; absorb her fleshy particulars and lavish nut-brown hair the photographers merely captured on a surface level.

This close, she was an intimidating presence: her nude-lips, aquiline nose, and winged eyeliner suggestive of a hieroglyph sprung to life.

Despite being cynical of top-tier celebrities in the past, Jaison could presently fathom her admirers' infatuation.

He said, 'Those legal aids. I imagine they would have divulged a lot more about me?'

Again that mischievous, playful smile.

'They did. They also revealed that during your formative years in Australia, those years hanging out with local bands, you drank. Progressively, you became an alcoholic.'

An admission on his part, Jaison simply nodded.

'Fast forward a few years, and cognitive behavioral therapy taught you a life of complete abstinence. From what I understand, you've been sober for ten years.'

'Eleven,' he said absently, the number itself

like a prayer.

'In this house, my husband and I both drink, in addition to some staff. Sparingly, I might add. And you'll find wine is a constant at dinner. While alcohol is present, you have my word you'll never be offered a glass. My sister Harriet, whom I'm sure you've read about, has fought her own battles with addiction. Over the years, I've learned what works and what doesn't.'

'I appreciate that, I do. But being powerless isn't part of the equation anymore.'

Arabella favored this with a wry look. Seemingly on a roll now, she continued, 'You've been married twice. Once when you were nineteen, then again at twenty-seven. The first one was swiftly annulled … and the second, while somewhat successful, ended in a bitter separation and divorce.'

With Arabella's spiel, Jaison waited for past events to surface: memories latticed with discomfiture and shame.

Surprisingly, he felt none of those things.

'There are no children in your life to speak of, although your second wife Marion had a miscarriage. It weighs on you, but not heavily. Children were not something you envisioned for yourself when you were younger. By and large, the man Jaison Winters is a loner – someone who's happiest left to his own devices. Your remaining family, your older brother and younger sister, consider you a somewhat selfish man because of this trait.'

With a few bold sentences, a stranger was pulling apart his character and history. Outwardly,

Jaison felt he should be taken aback – Arabella's behind-the-scenes snooping had potentially crossed a line. No doubt, her hired help had used considerable clout to summon records and even speak to people who knew him …

Tactics out of reach for the average citizen.

Jaison *should* feel infringed upon.

And yet he didn't.

Because I would have done the same thing in her shoes.

Turning away and moving toward a window, Arabella said, 'I see you can appreciate my choices. Not only am I inviting an outsider into my home, you're someone who is going to be spending time with my children. My *children*, Jaison. I value them more than life.'

'I understand. If you hadn't done your homework on me, you'd have been neglectful. And that's something someone in your shoes can ill afford to do.'

'Thoroughly vetting someone … it's the only way to ensure our privacy. When I think about some of the security issues we've faced in the past, even from people I thought I could trust …'

The statement piqued Jaison's curiosity.

'So, this brings up the question,' he said. 'Why me? Surely there's some other journalist out there, one you've met before and trust? Why not partner with them instead?'

Arabella whirled, the physical action self-assured and forceful.

'Because I'm someone who trusts *myself*. A drive which has gotten me where I am today. For my first authorized biography, my gut instinct tells me *you* are the right person for the job. Jaison, do you have any questions for me tonight?'

More than you could possibly imagine. But let's start with something fun.

'Vanita mentioned the castle has its share of ghosts. Is there any truth to it?'

Arabella laughed. 'You're wondering if you'll have trouble sleeping at night?'

'Will I?'

'Any house like this has stories, of course. And I admit everyone here has had their brush with something strange. Are you familiar with any of them? I don't suppose Declan mentioned anything of its sordid past? Occasionally, he likes to play tour guide with new guests.'

Rising up in Jaison's mind's eye, a ballroom filled with hundreds of mannequins in a state of merriment. 'On the way up. We passed some black and white pictures.'

'You must mean Owen Headley's. Now *there's* a man who had an artist's eye.'

'Declan mentioned he was completely crazy.'

'Oh, he was crazy all right,' Arabella admitted. 'But I've often found, at least in my line of work, it's the eccentric among us who see into other worlds.'

'I actually agree with you. The same could be said for my tribe.'

'Did Declan say anything about … suicide brides?'

'He did not.'

'Just *one* of Oaklyn's stories. And this one's no

urban legend.'

Jaison's interest, mild to begin with, began to bourgeon.

'Jennifer and Amy were a female couple who married at Oaklyn in 1975. It was forbidden love, of course – same-sex nuptials not being recognized by New York State at the time. So, their ceremony was supposed to be entirely symbolic. Anyway, the manor had slowly become a place where people could celebrate their lifestyle without fear of judgment, a place where taboos could be explored.'

The words summoned more images for Jaison: extravagant parties attended by the crème de la crème of old Hollywood and the political elite. In these soirées, bacchanalia and sin were the order of the day.

'The girls were married on the lawn in a private affair, and both chose full bridal attire. Deciding their honeymoon would be here, Jennifer and Amy spent two nights sequestered together in a room on the third floor, number 119. On the third night of their stay, Amy took her own life.'

Preoccupied with the novelty of his new digs, Jaison abruptly felt the weight of them; Oaklyn Castle as a kind of living thing pressing down from above.

While it was true world events of import had taken place inside the mansion – hitman once taking out a powerful figure in the parking lot, among other things – these often paled in comparison to the minor human dramas of guests, many of which had also ended in tragedy.

Jaison asked, 'How did she … how did it

happen?'

'Still wearing her bridal veil, Amy hung herself from the balcony. And ten years later, on the anniversary of the day, Jennifer booked the same room and decided to follow suit.'

'What do you mean?'

'She hung herself in exactly the same manner.'

Suicide brides, Jaison thought. *Hence their name*.

More images ensued, these far more detailed than prodigal parties.

A young girl wrapped in a bridal veil, her engorged and purple face smeared with hurriedly applied makeup. Swaying in a breeze, stockings adored this girl's lower half, her shoes having fallen away when the noose snapped taunt.

Arabella could see him wrestling with the tale's specifics.

She said, 'I'm telling you not to scare you, only filling you in on some of the house's darker aspects. My daughter Selena, a budding writer herself, finds the stories positively delightful. Perhaps with the intention of writing her own book about Oaklyn one day, she's begun collecting a scrapbook of newspaper clippings. It's something she keeps secret.'

'I'll ask her about her writing ambitions. Oh … Declan mentioned something about a tour tomorrow?'

At this, his host's expression darkened into something else: apprehension and unease.

Maybe she isn't quite ready to have a stranger gallivanting around her castle yet.

Though her next words gave a lie to this and made Jaison see it was just the opposite.

'That was the original plan, yes. But I've decided otherwise. Tomorrow, I want you to roam the house and its outlying grounds at your own leisure. Some parts remain off limits … the horse stables, for example, empty as they are. But almost everything else – the gardens, the swimming pools will be free for you to explore. My family and I, we want you to feel completely at home. We want this to be a place you never want to leave.'

2

Notes: The Authorized Biography of Arabella Jaqus.

Darkness has descended on Oaklyn Castle; it presses against the windows, so I can see little outside. The only illumination is a kind of white mist or stagnant fog.

At this hour, not even the pond is visible.

***

No, this isn't the beginning of an epic ghost story – only the scribblings of a fatigued writer who will use these ongoing notes to lay the foundation of a nonfiction novel.

And what is this factual novel about?

Put succinctly, it is the story of arguably the most famous woman on the planet: her past, present, and future. A woman who has chosen me – ageing, mediocre me – for the task.

An undertaking I've accepted with no word yet on a publisher.

Not solely content to do a series of one-on-one interviews, Arabella flew me halfway across the country to Huntington, Long Island, and invited me to stay as a guest in her home.

And such a home it is!

Where to begin with first impressions?

Oaklyn Castle is as much as I envisioned it: part English manor, part French chateau, part medieval mansion from a more neoclassical time. While the building itself is ancient (built at the turn of the previous century), the upkeep I've observed is quite extraordinary.

As if everything from the skirting boards to the light fixtures were installed mere months ago.

That said, there is also a strange energy to the house, a type of charisma neither altogether pleasant nor welcoming.

Though such an atmosphere does not spring from its past history, which the caregiver and Arabella have broached – no, it seems to come from the walls itself.

Like the bricks and timbers are the body of a malign old man itching to do some harm.

Here I sit, writing about Oaklyn.

And neglecting the people inside.

Which Declan cautioned me against.

Do not make the mansion your focal point.

So for now, I won't.

What do I think about my host?

For the most part, my observations are in league with my previous preconceptions: Arabella is a stalwart of beauty and intelligence.

Self-conscious of her awesome standing, she compensates this awareness with a kind of apathetic and easy-going manner – quick to release a sly smile or subtle joke. I suspect that beneath the exterior (as seems common with many celebrities), there lurks a tortured being; a person whose ability to perceive the world so keenly puts her at odds with it. While other journalists have noticed this 'tortured artist' aspect – some have speculated Arabella has a history of self-harm – I personally don't think her character is that clearcut.

It's more an ... earnestness in the shine of her eyes.

A polish that declares Arabella Jaqus has ridden waves of melancholy mortals like me have only sampled.

It is my fervent wish – in the nights ahead – she will visit this room just as she did tonight.

And each successive conversation will knock down barriers the superstar has spent a lifetime cultivating.

And the others?

This early, there is little to know.

The caregiver – Declan Avery – appears to be

pleasant and outwardly loyal to the family.

The twins (Vanita and Kingston) are intelligent and well mannered, their vocabulary and intellect above average for their age. An observer could attribute this to their home schooling, but I hazard it may come simply from rubbing shoulders with creative behemoths in the film industry; Arabella's peers who in all probability accord them a certain respect because of the veneration granted to the family.

Including their father, Boyd Palmer.

Ghost Dad, Vanita named him.

Noticeably absent today, the trappings of Boyd Palmer's lucrative career take him away for weeks, sometimes months at a time.

Will he put in a prolonged visit during my stay?

Will I get to know Arabella and Boyd's secret chemistry away from the plastic varnish of magazine spreads?

Unfortunately, my host hasn't been altogether forthcoming on particulars, being somewhat extemporaneous on my role here. An example of this is deciding to let me have free reign of the castle, exploring its myriad rooms on my own.

A task I will begin tomorrow.

No doubt, these wanderings will introduce me to her adopted children, all of whom seem to have their own private space relative to their respective interests.

And who knows ... maybe I'll meet a few ghosts.

Through a pocket in my jeans, I can feel the weight of Vanita's gift.

Her Nazar Boncuk.

A talisman designed to protect me from the dark.

3

Night in Oaklyn.

From the hallway beyond Jaison's room, footsteps interrupt sporadic dreams.

Awakening, it takes some time before his eyes can adjust to a shrouded environment alien to his familiar surrounds.

Footsteps come to a rest.

Then his door begins to open.

Feeling too sleep-addled to be scared, Jaison elevates himself upright.

Her face obscured by some extension; a woman enters the room.

She's wearing a mask, he thinks. And on the heels of this: *I must still be dreaming.*

He must be.

Because the mask-adorned woman *also* wears bridal attire: a white arrangement of flowing sleeves flutter around structured satin.

A suicide bride?

Like a snout, an elongated protrusion sprouts from the mask of the veiled apparition. Retreating shadows reveal a person whose headdress is suggestive of a forbidden, phallic apparatus.

A bedroom toy.

Normally such a prospect would lean toward the comical, but the sight of this newlywed wearing an elephantine strap-on is ominous.

Silvered with moonlight, tufts of black hair bud from the woman's disguise like stuffing from a scarecrow.

I'm dreaming of the star-crossed lover from Arabella's tale?

As though reading his thought, the woman reaches out, her gnarled fingers making the shape of a claw.

***

Jaison opened his eyes to dawn's light.

Beyond the curtains, an overcast day lay sodden with clouds.

Supplementing the grey, a harried wind shrieked against windowpanes, rattling the timbers.

For several minutes he lay inert, relishing the softness of pillowcases and sheets that – in all probability – exceeded the cost of his wardrobe.

He was far away from his own bed and home, yes … but a freedom existed in these circumstances that made Jaison feel genuinely liberated.

Because outside these walls, a virus rages on. A respiratory thing called COVID-19 that in all likelihood will never be properly contained.

Oaklyn Castle, tucked far away from humanity's hordes, represented undeniable safety.

He was also shielded against humanity's toxic eternal politicking.

On any other morning, he would gravitate to his phone, there to access the overall state of the world through social media.

Today, he decided to abscond the phone entirely.

Thirty minutes later, showered and dressed, Declan Avery arrived to escort him down to the kitchen.

*****

As they walked, Declan asked, 'Did you sleep all right?'

'Fine. But I remember some … vivid dreams. I guess my subconscious decided to play around with stuff from a conversation I had.'

With morning, the specifics of Jaison's dreams were fading somewhat. Still, he *did* recall a bride and her entire form ornamented with some kind of ceremonial headdress …

'As long as they didn't feature mannequins. I'd

hate to be responsible for *that*.'

A short time later, having navigated two sets of stairs, Jaison heard the raised clatter of food preparation.

Declan led them into an expansive space containing three full kitchen islands, each one paired with respective chandeliers.

Sharing the first one, Arabella sat with Vanita. Their backs to the newcomers, an attractive black lady stood next to Kingston.

Perched on the second island was an Asian boy in his teens. Seeing Declan and Jaison emerge, his face broke out in a flippant grin.

'Another lamb to the slaughter,' he said, then chuckled. 'Well to breakfast, anyway. You must be our new writer. My name is Phuoc.'

From the opposite island, Vanita said, 'Mommy told us your name was spelt funny, with an i in the middle. Is this true?'

Without waiting for an invitation, Jaison took a seat next to Phuoc.

'It's true. I'm Jaison with an i. And it's something I always get asked about. I was named after my father, who is Irish. And no … I'm not Irish myself. I was born in Australia.'

'How can your daddy be Irish, but you were born in Australia?' Vanita asked. 'Is your daddy still alive?'

Arabella gave her daughter a disapproving

stare, but Jaison held up a hand.

'Quite all right. During the early Seventies, my mother went to Ireland on vacation. She *loved* the place, and I suspect would have moved there if money wasn't an obstacle. Anyway, she met a man named Jaison in Dublin, and they had a romantic adventure together. Afterward, they fell out of touch. When she came home, I was born …but the name stuck with her.'

'So, you never met your daddy?' Vanita asked. 'That's very sad.'

'Yes, it's sad. Interestingly, I was originally going to be called *Guthrie*. Dozens of Guthries walking around Ireland, I'm told. But my mother said not many of them were pleasant chaps.'

For whatever reason, this elicited a laugh from the woman next to Kingston. Turning around to face them, Jaison noticed she grasped a spatula.

Attractive wasn't quite the right adjective.

The woman was divine.

She said, 'I can vouch that not every Guthrie is pleasant. Cantankerous, old Catholic is probably a more fitting description for the one I knew.'

'Jaison,' said Arabella. 'May I introduce Ophelia Taylor. Ophelia and I have been friends for half a lifetime … and she's been our personal chef for half the twins' lifetime.'

'Once upon a time,' Ophelia said. 'I was a makeup artist. That's where Arabella and I were first introduced.'

In between sips of coffee from a ceramic mug, Arabella said, 'It was on those early films I did for Paramount. Anyway, when you have your ass parked in a makeup chair for hours, you get to know the people you work with pretty intimately.'

'I was never that good at applying foam rubber or latex,' Ophelia said. 'Definitely much better cooking for the crew and lighting up Arabella's cigarettes. Speaking of … what would you like to eat this morning, Jaison? Kingston has been helping me make French toast.'

'Sounds perfect,' he replied, both his reaction and words feeling abruptly dreamlike.

Appreciate the moment. Because a week ago, your ex-wife called you a washed-up has-been. Now the hired help of a movie star is about to make you French toast.

A surreal moment was complimented by an undeniable energy that felt comfortably commonplace.

A loving family enjoying each other's company.

Beside him, Phuoc said, 'My brother mentioned you've written some horror books. Have any of them been turned into a movie?'

'I've written *one* horror book. Some critics have pointed out it's a poor attempt at the genre. Unfortunately, no. Nothing I've written has been given the film treatment.'

Having taken a seat next to Declan, Kingston said, 'Maybe Mom can help you out with that. I'm not sure if you're aware, but she has a *lot* of pull in Hollywood.'

General laughter erupted, and Jaison joined in.

Kingston made a joke, but Jaison held up his hand again. 'Any writer alive, including me, would gladly take advantage of who you know to get something adapted. But I'm afraid a book like *Parasites* just isn't up to snuff.'

Giggling, Vanita said, 'Up to *snuff*?'

'It basically means not good enough. *Parasites* was written a long time ago when evil dolls and such were all the rage. While the book has a few fans, I feel the world has moved on.'

'Like Chucky, you mean?' asked Kingston. 'You wrote a book like Chucky the evil doll?'

'Not … quite like Chucky. My creatures were a little different – sort of mischievous and fun. More like Gremlins.'

'I love those films,' said Phuoc. 'Mogwais are the best.'

In the act of placing plates down among the sitting, Ophelia said, 'Did you happen to bring a copy of *Parasites* with you? I might like to read it.'

'I think the paperback is out of print, unfortunately. Just a few expensive copies floating around on eBay. But if you have no aversion to eBooks –'

'No need for eBooks,' said Arabella. 'I've made sure Oaklyn's library has its very own Jaison Winters section. Everything you've penned, alphabetically arranged. Which reminds me … perhaps you'd like to make the library your first port of call today? It's got everything, of course – from the fictional greats to medical books dating back to the fifteenth century. Did you know the original architect installed a type of fireman's pole? You can slide down it from one level to the next.'

Everyone was watching him expectantly – Jaison was momentarily at a loss to reply. A bibliophile for most of his remembered life, granted the knowledge a fireman's pole existed in any library was a revelation.

And knowing the same library housed his own collection was even more startling.

Don't forget Arabella has read every word. I wonder how long it will take her to ask if the alcoholic protagonist of Parasites *is based on your good self.*

He said, 'Sounds like a plan.'

'Good. Declan can take you there after breakfast.'

Silent since entering, Jaison had almost forgotten the caregiver was present.

He observed he was not eating, seemed completely oblivious of everything except …

The makeup artist turned chef.

To ascertain he was observing a man with a crush, Jaison didn't need to be an expert on body language.

Appearing spellbound, Declan gazed at the object of his affection as if Ophelia were the sole human alive.

Smiling and laughing, she appeared unaware there was a suitor in her midst.

Or perhaps they have a history together.

More talk ensued, everything from Kingston's latest math test to Vanita's current obsession with frogs.

And her desire for a large aquarium in which to raise an army of them.

Arabella, not acquiescing nor entirely ruling out the prospect, left the door open to future amphibians if Vanita showed an aptitude for fostering them.

In addition to improving her own math.

Throughout, the writer took mental notes, meditated on chapters that would accurately chronicle this family dynamic.

***

They were on the third floor, halfway down a hallway, when Declan's phone chimed.

A look of grave concern came over his

normally placid features.

'I'm needed. Something that can't be avoided.'

Jaison studied the hallway, abruptly feeling as troubled as Declan looked.

'Should I wait for you?'

'No need. When you get to the end of this hallway, turn right. Then follow it down. At the very end you'll see two giant mahogany things – the doors to the library.'

Jaison noted Declan's mind was already elsewhere, solving whatever complicated issue beset Arabella's twins.

Or perhaps his mistress only requires her laundry appraised. Menial tasks do not wait for those unused to waiting ...

'Okay,' said Jaison. 'Thanks for taking me this far.'

Declan loped down the hallway with the ambling gait of an Olympic race walker.

Leaving Jaison alone.

Covering the walls, Anglo-Japanese wallpaper was embossed with exotic motifs and asymmetrical designs.

As Declan instructed, Jaison walked to the far end and rounded the corner.

On the way, he passed seven separate rooms, their purposes unknown.

Though nobody was watching him, he decided not to open any doors.

A new, longer hallway presented itself. Toward its center, a decorative arch of painted columns served as more ornamentation. Angular rather than coiled, side curvatures formed decorative keystone surrounds.

Absently, Jaison pried out his cell, hit the recording app. He said, 'Parts of Oaklyn Castle appear … almost divorced from each other. Stepping from one hallway into another can be like stepping into a different house.'

Past the arch, another oddity: a floor-to-ceiling mirror supported by a tapered hood, its frame golden and gilded.

For a time, Jaison studied his reflection, observed something in his stare unforeseen.

Creased eyebrows asserted someone on edge.

Trepidation. Perhaps even fear?

It was subtle.

But certainly there.

Is it really that surprising? You've been left alone in a massive house more suggestive of a church or cathedral.

And large mirrors reflecting the ill-omened atmosphere did not help.

Before anything strange could transpire, he moved on from the mirror.

Soon, Declan's mahogany doors were revealed, their timber so polished he could perceive, as he approached, his likeness again.

These doors, like so many in Oaklyn, were inlaid with a filigree of ornate design.

Two brass knobs provided access.

Choosing the right door, Jaison stepped into the library of Oaklyn Castle.

***

Comparable to other depositories where books had a permanent home, it was their smell he noticed: a spicy aroma of parchment and leathers.

Pages that evoked (to Jaison, at least) the smell of fresh almonds and vanilla flowers.

He shut his eyes … and smiled simply for the sake of it.

Like coming home.

Opening them, the first thing to stand out was a spiral staircase, more custom mahogany millwork.

Two levels were augmented by double radius pocket doors.

Custom art glass illuminated a coiffured dome ceiling.

Books without covers occupied the immediate shelves he could see.

Near the middle of the first floor, couches composed of boiled wool and cashmere sat like inviting sentinels.

Where the first bookshelves ended, Jaison spotted a dove onyx fireplace.

Closer inspection exposed an artificial grate and logs within an authentic hearth.

An electric fire heater. Which makes perfect sense in the context of the environment.

For a moment he envisioned both books and mahogany being devoured by a conflagration that, once begun, could not be quenched.

'Don't bother trying to turn it on,' said a voice behind him. 'It hasn't worked since last winter.'

Jaison released a bent-up breath.

His trepidation, having abated since entering the library, remained in a heightened state.

A young girl stood by the staircase.

More a young woman. Someone just out of her teens, anyway.

Dark skin belied a similar linage to Ophelia.

Hands behind her back, the girl regarded Jaison with a sheepish smile.

He said, 'You scared me. You're not a ghost, are you?'

This produced a laugh, as exotic as the girl appeared.

'I don't think so. Flesh and blood all the way. Do I *look* like a ghost?'

'No. You look like Selena, Arabella's daughter. Would that be your name?'

'It would be. And you must be Mr. Winters. I was told I might bump into you.'

Much like Kingston and Vanita, the girl

possessed an educated cadence – her character almost bookish.

No surprise I would find her in the library ...

'So, what happens when it gets really cold in here? How do you stay warm and read with a fireplace on the blink?'

'Mr. Federer – Eden, I mean. Eden lets me call him by his first name. He will usually come along and repair it. In fact, he should soon, what with winter on the doorstep and all.'

'You can *also* call me by my first name. Who is Eden?'

'Eden is the closest thing to a handyman Oaklyn has. And he was fixing things here long before I came along. Although … he's not around much anymore. I think it has something to do with Amelia.'

Already Selena was disclosing things Jaison was ignorant of; material he'd like to record. Of course, he wouldn't do that.

Bad etiquette.

'I haven't met Amelia yet. Declan mentioned she's a gardener?'

Selena nodded. 'Mostly. She sleeps in the old chapel. A few years ago, she and Eden were dating, like boyfriend and girlfriend. From what I know, their relationship did not end well.'

'I see.'

An uncomfortable silence ensued, one where

Jaison noticed Selena's hands weren't visible because they clutched something behind her back.

A book.

Selena said, 'The lift is out of order as well. But that's something Eden won't be fixing now or ever.'

Jaison was astonished. 'I wasn't aware Oaklyn *had* a lift system. I've been using stairs since I arrived.'

'You've been using them because Daddy and Momma forbid using the lift. It broke down shortly after we moved in, and they've decided to leave it broken.'

'Why, if I may ask?'

'Momma thinks it's too dangerous. For her children, anyway. She has nightmares about us getting stuck.'

'That's understandable.'

'With the house so far away from everything else, it would take some time for help to arrive. Oaklyn used to have *two* lifts … which I read about in a book. I read all kinds of books.'

Beaming, Jaison said, 'So do I. They're an addiction. Your mom mentioned you like to study up on Oaklyn's past – and sometimes you like to write stories?'

Having ignited something within the girl, Selena's smile was also genial. She said, 'There was another famous movie star who lived here in the

Twenties. Did you know that? Her husband, who was sometimes abusive, shot himself in the head while standing in front of a mirror.'

A mirror, thought Jaison, and cast his mind back to the hallway. *No prizes for guessing which one.*

'A butler found him first. But instead of calling the police, he called a film studio. Of course, there were rumors it wasn't a suicide. Many who were staying here said it was his mistress who pulled the trigger.'

'Why would they think that?'

'Because she jumped off a boat to her death only a few days later.'

In tone, the tale was like Arabella's suicide brides, a bygone tragedy of ill-begotten love.

Though it was on the tip of his tongue to know the identity of the movie star, he instead asked: 'Is that story in one of these books? Are there any about Oaklyn Castle itself you could show me?'

Selena's amiable smile turned mischievous.

This was a girl who had her own secret world.

'Momma had most of those books removed. She said they were becoming harmful to me. She said they were the reason I had trouble sleeping.'

'Were they?'

'No. Well, I *was* having trouble sleeping. But it wasn't because of a book about this house. My brother, Montha, he sometimes likes to scare me.'

'How so?'

A forlorn look came over the girl, and she shrugged the question away.

'It doesn't matter. There's no books, but there's tons of information in some of the old newspapers. They're kept on the second floor. I can show them to you.'

Old newspapers; a written portal into Oaklyn's past.

The prospect filled Jaison with anticipation.

She's lonely. Wants to share her inner world with someone she's just met.

And there was little doubt Selena could sense Jaison's own inquisitiveness; a type of journalistic avarice he'd always worn like an invisible badge.

'I would like that. Newspapers … let's just say they'll help with my project.'

'The project you're doing on my family?'

Jaison gave a lopsided grin. 'The very one. But today – perhaps you can just show me around the library? Your mom told me earlier some of my own books are here.'

'Second floor,' said Selena.

After placing her book on an armrest, Selena began negotiating the spiral staircase, Jaison close behind. For balance, small balustrades were affixed to the risers, their lower portion finished in a pendent-drop motif. At the summit, a large newel post with faceted carvings served as an introduction to the second floor.

On this level, grand scale bookcases were interwoven with artisanal cabinetry.

Three separate ladders gave access to the bookcases.

'Look up,' Selena instructed, then pointed to the domed ceiling above. 'See those designs? They were inspired by a church in France, the Cathedral Basilica of Saint Cecelia. And over there …' Selena's hand gravitated toward the east wall. 'A local artist at Momma's bidding inscribed Latin verses onto the walls.'

Latin verses in old English font were indeed impressive, yet they paled in comparison to the west wall.

Which featured a grand mahogany wet bar complete with wine cooler.

Selena noticed the bar had Jaison's full attention.

'There are antique books behind the bar,' he said.

'Books about beer. One of the largest collections in the country. They were donated by the World Brewing Academy.'

Jaison licked his lips. 'I don't drink anymore … but seeing this, I almost lament the decision.'

This admission seemed to catch his guide by surprise.

'You don't? I assumed all writers drank. I'll

have to remember that.'

Jaison, wanting to change the subject, pointed to the closest shelves. 'What kind of books are on this wall? Are they all leather bound?'

'Mainly nonfiction. Architecture, folklore, the history of Long Island. The kind of thing my dad loves. Further down there's food, wine, and fashion. The kind of thing *Momma* loves.'

Hearing mention of Boyd Palmer caused Jaison to slow his stride. An enigma possessing elusive qualities (at least from afar), it was difficult to imagine the celebrity doing something routine like spending time in a library.

And even harder to imagine him parenting this child.

Again on the cusp of broaching a subject best ignored, Jaison was relieved to be interrupted by something Arabella had teased: a fireman's pole, as gilded as the sides of a mirror.

Grinning, Selena said, 'Trumps the spiral staircase, don't you think?'

'Was it always a part of the library?'

'From what I know, it was drawn into the original designs for Oaklyn. While I personally use it on occasion, a fireman's pole doesn't need to be functional to serve its purpose. This one reflects the *personality* of the house, I think. Reinforces an industrial-chic vibe.'

Jaison laughed. 'Industrial chic, huh?'

'Interior design that takes an inspiration from factories and industrial spaces. You see, Daddy isn't the only one in our family who has an interest in architecture.'

Around the pole, a steel partition served as a makeshift barrier for the circular cavity. Jaison watched as Selena walked up to the railing, placed her fingers along the top and peered down.

She said, 'I need to get back to my room.'

'So soon?'

'The book I found today – it didn't reveal much of anything. So, I'm going to do some research on my computer.'

With that, the girl manhandled her frame over the barrier.

'Momma placed your own books in the nonfiction section. I haven't read any, sorry. It was a pleasure to meet you, Jaison. I do hope we see each other again.'

Without waiting for a reply, Selena latched onto the fireman's pole.

And disappeared.

***

He felt bewildered.

Not only had Selena's introduction been short, but he'd also been deprived of asking her certain questions.

For instance, what book failed to reveal anything? Was there something she was studying or researching?

Private questions. You're here to learn about them, not interrogate them.

And yet …

He'd been appointed *scribe* for the family living under this roof; he had been given permission to begin a dialogue. If he couldn't get to the meat of their separate personalities now, then when was it expected?

'Perhaps when you're settled more,' he said to the empty library. 'It's not like you're working against a deadline.'

Almost as an afterthought, he made his way to the bar.

Moments later he sat perched upright on a stool, gazing at a menagerie of alcoholic beverages – bottles gleaming with ripples of light.

Arabella conveyed something during her bedroom visit. What was it?

While alcohol is present, you have my word you'll never be offered a glass.

Presently, Jaison didn't need to be offered anything.

He could just stand, walk up to a row, and help himself to a bottle of black label *Johnny Walker*.

Watch it splash into a clean glass full of ice cubes …

Deprived of such luxuries for over a decade now, whiskey would slide slick down an eager gullet.

His thoughts, which began innocently enough, were suddenly a cause for concern.

What the hell am I thinking?

His staunch sobriety, a hard-won thing years in the making, was now in jeopardy because he stood alone in front of a stocked bar?

These questions invariably led back to memories of drinking; snippets of recollection played like grainy footage on an old projector.

Jaison Winters arriving at a liquor store precisely at opening time, his fingers jittering. Because if he didn't get some booze into his system *yesterday*, a withdrawal seizure was potentially in the offing.

Jaison Winters abusing his ex-wife verbally because she'd had the *audacity* to ask him to stop.

Dark times you don't need to put under a microscope. You're a different man, now.

Yes, he was.

A bona-fide nondrinker.

And what did nondrinkers do?

They stayed the hell away from bars squirrelled away in opulent libraries.

With a sigh of resignation, Jaison abandoned the bar stool.

***

He found his own collection where Selena declared it would be: twenty-one titles in nonfiction, lined up in order of publication.

Like an itemized graph showcasing the peaks and troughs of his own weary career.

The first novels, first editions in hardback, exhibited such titles as *Waiting for the Sun* and *Rock and Roll's Legendary Neighborhood*. Toward the middle, more middling fare in the form of *The True Adventures of Solid State*.

It was near the end, however, where things became unscrupulous; the designations mirroring a seedy and self-loathing realm Jaison occupied at the time: *Hammer of the Gods*, *Please Kill Me*, and *Lonely Boy: Tales of A Punk Band*.

His one stab at genre fiction, *Parasites*, served as a bookend to the whole collection.

For Jaison Sebastian Winters, there were no children to speak of; no stories of family or domestic adventures he could regal.

There were only these sordid words.

A chronicling of other lives far more fantastical than his own.

But you had fun with those bands. Got to hang out and party with the best of them. Doesn't that count for something?

It might ... if Jaison could recall some of those

parties. As it stood, his overall remembrance was occluded by a miasma of blackouts.

Of making writing deadlines solely because he was hopped up on speed.

His brooding thoughts were suddenly disturbed.

By a sound like scurrying.

The click of paws.

Has Selena returned?

No, the scampering sound issued from further back, close to bookshelves by the bar.

More skittering.

Jaison turned around.

And spotted something like an appendage slipping between shelves.

Did Arabella own pets?

Most large families possessed them.

Up until now, Jaison had not inquired about animals.

Besides Vanita voicing her desire for frogs, he'd not encountered a single domestic animal either roaming the hallways or lounging on a couch.

So, what was between the shelves?

Bereft of any noticeable fur, he'd glimpsed a blur of grey flesh.

Keeping his body idle, Jaison held his breath.

Hoping a lack of sound or visible movement would serve as a vacuum to absorb *other* sounds.

The scampering did not come again.

Deciding to tread softly, he moved toward the offending shelf, skulking with a ballerina's finesse.

A short distance from where the appendage had disappeared, golden eyes regarded him.

In this quiet space, the sight of something *alive* caused Jaison to totter, triggered his heartbeat again.

Perhaps the visitor was of no more import than wandering vermin.

A large rat.

Or potentially an opossum.

In the interest of pacifying the creature, Jaison decided to simply retreat.

From its eyes came a strange species of malevolence.

And its clicking sounds resumed.

As though the creature, in a bull's manner, prepared to charge.

The image finally broke his paralysis.

Without breaking eye contact, Jaison backtracked toward the fireman's pole.

Reaching it, he observed something emerge from the niche, a thing whose frontal physiognomy contained a spittle-slicked mouth.

As swiftly as Selena, Jaison disappeared down the pole.

***

Despite the above threat, he felt secure back on

the first floor.

His first instinct: make a beeline for the mahogany exit.

Except something on the cashmere couch demanded Jaison's attention.

Selena's book.

Aware that garish movement might alert his upstairs visitor, he crept toward the hardback and claimed it.

Held its cover up to the light.

The title was: *Haitian Vodou*.

While anticipating something outlandish, this particular subject matter came as a surprise.

On the dust jacket, a ceremonial garbed priest stared out at Jaison with malign, bloodshot eyes.

Only an illustration (an artist's interpretation), the dark priest wore the hooded expression of someone who takes pleasure from another person's pain.

Directly above, a shifting reverberation pierced the silence.

The sound of something far removed from claws.

Still holding the novel, Jaison sprinted toward the doors.

***

Exiting, there was no reason to presume

anything else untoward would follow him out.

So seeing a suited *man* standing by the hallway mirror, he froze.

Facing away and staring at his reflection, the grey-haired man held a gun in his left hand.

Slowly, he lifted the weapon to his temple.

Deigning not to turn around, the stranger only had eyes for his mirror self.

Countless questions arose.

Chief among them: Who was this stranger?

Jaison could not deny there was also a feeling of wonder – curiosity spiked at the seams with mounting dread.

Because this exact scene had been described to him a short time ago.

Selena's tale of suicide.

As though receiving instructions from the mirror, the man lowered his gun, then raised it.

Lowered, then raised again.

Jaison noticed his three-piece suit contained a spark of red; floral decoration attached to a pleated white shirt.

Closer examination of his attire revealed a bow tie and gloves.

The kind of apparel befitting someone from an older era.

Or a character penned by a jazz-age novelist like F. Scott Fitzgerald.

Again, the gun was raised … and Jaison

retreated two steps.

Without pausing to consider his actions, he slammed the door, hand gripping the knob so firmly his fingers were drained of color.

He was about to do it.

How he knew this as a certainty was unclear – instinct screamed no hesitation remained in the stranger.

His reluctance had come to an end.

Poised against a mahogany frame, Jaison heard no shot from the other side.

On the first and second floor of Oaklyn's library, there was only silence.

Oaklyn, Jaison thought.

A place where mysterious creatures skulked.

And ghosts cavorted in corridors.

No – don't do that. Don't give it a label. It was just an ordinary man …. or the family is attempting to scare you. In fact, you were probably summoned for their own amusement. A plaything for the rich and bored.

He counted to ten.

Reaching twenty, he manhandled the knob with trembling fingers – ready to greet whatever waited outside.

Motes of dust, the sole movement, drifted in serried shafts of grey light from a diffuse sky.

No stranger stood in the hallway.

4

<u>Notes: The Authorized Biography of Arabella Jaqus.</u>

Before penning these words, I've briefly gone over those preceding them, my first entry of thoughts less than twenty-four hours ago.

I discovered a sentence near the end reading: And who knows … maybe I'll meet a few ghosts.

***

The question is: Did I meet one today?
I'm not entirely sure.
But I know one thing.
Twenty-four hours can feel like a lifetime.
Night has again laid claim to Oaklyn Castle, and though many things have transpired, I didn't get to explore much of the house.
Certainly not as much as I desired.
After my encounter in the library and

subsequently in the hallway, I returned promptly to these rooms.

Here to while away the hours, thinking and writing.

There is a lot to think about.

At my request (I texted Arabella on a private number she provided), lunch and dinner were brought up to my rooms by Ophelia. While the resident chef was amiable toward me, we did not engage in any conversation besides formal pleasantries. True to the woman I met this morning, Ophelia has a welcoming and homely personality; not only do I feel completely at ease in her company, but I feel the door is open for me to ask all manner of questions.

Except perhaps the question I want to ask the most.

What is her personal experience with the supernatural inside Oaklyn Castle?

Maybe this is something I can broach later, when I have a better understanding of what – if anything – I experienced today.

There are different likelihoods, and I have not ruled out the possibility that Jaison Winters is indeed some kind of toy, bidden here by a family of pranksters who would like to observe my reaction to ghost stories made manifest.

Besides the elusive Montha, I have now met all of Arabella's children.

Including Selena, the bookish scholar who, while I preferred additional time with, divulged more material than the others combined.

Of course, it stands to reason she was potentially feeding me falsehoods, parceling out another story of death, so there would be no mistaking who I glimpsed in the hallway evaluating his own reflection.

And what of the strange golden-eyed apparition which – pains me to admit – somehow felt familiar?

The overriding question is this: Do I play a game of ignorance as I continue to explore the remainder of Oaklyn Castle?

While I have no proof of what occurred in the library, I did bring back a single keepsake – something I held onto almost as an unconscious afterthought. Presently it sits beside these handwritten pages, a book on Haitian Voodoo that Selena held for reasons I hope to know.

One interesting thing: Arabella and Boyd's other child, Montha, was adopted from an orphanage in Haiti – the third largest country in the Caribbean Sea.

Montha, whom I'm yet to meet.

According to the twins, he's a teenager who spends much of his time outside.

A place where he can work on personal projects.

Whatever that means.

Speaking of the mother ...

Tonight, she did not pay me a visit.

Previously I remained hopeful our conversations would be an ongoing thing – I'm certain now they won't be. For some reason, Arabella desires I discover things in a journalistic fashion: seek out the story like a reporter digging for the truth. Like others here, there is an aspect to my presence beyond that of hired help, but I'm still beneath the taciturn gaze of a boss who sits on the throne of celebrity.

So, I will grant her wish.

Tomorrow morning, I plan to scout the external environs of this magnificent castle ... abandon the interior and see what marvels exist on the outside.

There are gardens, of course – and greenhouses – but some instinct tells me Oaklyn Castle has much more to show me than the standard mansions of old.

5

Lashing windows and sputtering down gutters, morning rain drummed upon the roof as if battalions of opposing armies were in conflict.

Outside, the mansion's pond had flooded its banks.

Jaison thought: *My outside explorations will have to wait.*

Through a window, he could discern the pond as something semi-transparent, almost wraithlike. Beneath this gauze, there was no sign of the decorative vines he'd glimpsed the previous day.

After some time staring, he spied a human figure.

The shape was small in stature; Jaison might have missed it altogether if not for the hooded outline.

The silhouette of somebody wearing an olive-green rain slicker.

Vanita, he thought.

Which stood to reason.

Because Declan mentioned the girl had claimed

the pond as her own.

Groom Lake.

A nickname for her private playground.

Their back to Oaklyn Castle (and Jaison's window), the hooded figure swayed when buffeted by a deluge of wind-swept rain.

Would Arabella let her daughter play near the pond in this weather?

Though the notion was farfetched, he thought it feasible.

Because these people, this family, were still strangers to him.

Games in the rain were potentially as commonplace as hide and seek, as conventional as kick the can in decades past.

After three more minutes of studying the figure, Jaison was prepared to abandon his watch.

Whomever they were, gaped at the undulating surface of a rain-pummeled pond – an activity that might occupy them all morning.

Abruptly, the figure turned around.

Stared straight up at Jaison's position behind the window.

Dirty shadows hidden within a windbreaker; a black smudge for a face.

Not Vanita.

No, this couldn't be. The person was midget-sized, a dwarfish apparition who glowered upwards as if fully aware Jaison was the first one observing.

No human face was discernable inside that smudge of shadow.

Fleet of foot, the figure suddenly *leapt* forward, scampering toward the house.

Heart pounding, Jaison retreated.

Withdrew back toward his bed.

Where dreams of a mirror man plagued his sleep the night before.

***

Noon came and with its arrival the skies around Oaklyn Castle cleared. This swift change in weather – operatic rain to placid sunshine – somehow felt like an echo of the house itself.

Unnerving one moment.

Beguiling the next.

Having spent the remainder of his morning drinking coffee and writing, Jaison Winters took the change of climate as a sign to leave his room and venture outside.

***

To find an appropriate exit, he did not require a tour guide.

On the first floor, a nondescript door provided admission to a courtyard teeming with gardenia and grass.

Droplets of dew were the only evidence of the morning's deluge.

Beyond the courtyard, sandstone steps gave way to wider spaces of landscaping more akin to the veldt of a tennis court.

Walking, Jaison contemplated the pond. Considered the childlike figure standing by its edge.

A shadow face within an olive-green hood ...

Withdrawing from the window, Jaison had not returned, sure in the knowledge that whatever their identity was, they were cognizant of his spying.

But I wasn't spying. I was just admiring the view.

Still.

He was a guest here.

He was not (and never would be) someone who lived within the walls of the castle.

For those who *did* live here, it was natural for them to feel a certain ownership: one deserving of the privacy they were accustomed.

Of course, niggling in the back of his mind was a theory, a supposition, that perhaps the rain-slicked midget wasn't a resident at all.

Perhaps they were of the same ilk as the mirror man.

A phantom ... here one moment, gone the next.

Surely not.

Because Jaison recalled rain bouncing off the jacket.

Even from his third floor, this effect had been visible.

Some distance from the house now, lawns gave way to low hillocks. To guide him, a makeshift path wove between sugar maple trees.

When Jaison walked into the heart of this small arboreal realm, he was shocked to discover water fountains.

Three of them, replete with pissing cherubs.

And beside the center fountain stood Ophelia Taylor.

Her back to Jaison, she remained unaware of his approach.

It was a picturesque tableau, and for a few seconds Jaison simply admired it. The cherubs, arrow wielders, wore expressions mischievous and somehow amorous. Her left hand brokering the water's surface, Ophelia's sun-spangled hair glistened as though oiled.

Taking a single step forward, a twig broke beneath Jaison's shoe.

Ophelia looked back, startled.

Producing a lazy smile, she said, 'It's you. This morning I didn't think the rain was going to relent. Luckily it did … and now we have a perfect afternoon.'

'Why I decided to venture out,' he said, then inched closer to the fountain. 'Though I admit … I don't really know where I'm headed.'

'Thought you'd just wing it?'

'Pretty much. And enjoy the surprises that come.'

'That's the beauty of Oaklyn, if you ask me.'

'What is?'

'It's full of surprises.'

Not really, he thought. *Most people arrive here thinking the house is haunted. And most people would be right.*

Still wearing an indolent smile, Ophelia sat down on the edge of the fountain. She said, 'This is one of my favorite places to visit. Just to think.'

Jaison studied the jets of water containing colorful prisms. 'Nothing to hear but trickling water. It's beautiful.'

'But not the kind of place someone like you would do their best thinking, I suspect. That would be in a library, yes? How did it go yesterday? It's quite the environment, isn't it?'

Thinking of something with gold-rimmed eyes wedged between shelves, Jaison said nothing. By degrees, he quelled the image.

'It was everything I imagined. How many libraries do you see with a bar these days?'

Ophelia laughed. 'That's what everybody mentions first. You'd think it would be the skylight, the fireman's pole, or the vast book collection. But no.'

In between his own giggles, Jaison said, 'Can I

ask you something, Ophelia? Has anything occurred in that library that you'd personally deem … uncanny?'

Ophelia appeared genuinely confused. 'What do you mean?'

Now you've gone and done it. Made yourself look foolish before you've had meaningful conversations with the chef.

He said, 'When you're alone in there … it felt like I was in this silent, separate world. Have you ever experienced anything a bit weird or out of the ordinary?'

She nodded as if she knew *precisely* what he was talking about. 'People mention the bar – yet they *also* allude to the overall vibe. Personally, I haven't spent all that much time in there. My realm has always been the kitchen.'

Feeling as if Ophelia had a punchline in the wings, Jaison fell silent again. After a while, his patience was rewarded.

'I *did* hear one thing. And I think it was Amelia who first told me. Early last century, when construction of the library began, the builders discovered an unmarked burial mound. An actual grave containing the skeletons of an adult and two children. Their bones were … very old. They were donated to a local university for study. Later, they revealed the child skeletons had been twins, a boy and a girl. The adult, their mother.'

As a story, it was somewhat disappointing. Eagerly, Jaison had been anticipating something of the poltergeist variety.

Or an anecdote that would echo Selena's story of suicide.

His very own mirror man.

Then he apprehended there *was* an echo of the present.

In the previous century, even before the building's construction, twins had perished here.

And twins held court in Oaklyn Castle today …

Jaison asked, 'Do you know how old the siblings were?'

Suddenly, despite these peaceable surroundings, he wanted to get moving again. Amelia, her name mentioned numerous times now, was somebody he wanted to meet.

'They weren't infants, if that's what you mean. Selena would be the one to glean that information from. Oh … I understand you two were introduced to each other yesterday?'

Word travels quickly.

'We were – briefly. She's a smart cookie.'

Red lipstick emphasizing exotic features, Ophelia's look was wistful. She said, 'She is indeed. So … may I ask what happened to you in there, Jaison Winters? What did you see that would prompt you to ask the question?'

Not anticipating the chef's brazenness, he was

momentarily lost for a reply. Then he fumbled for an explanation he had no intention of fully revealing.

'Well, what I *thought* I saw wasn't even in the library. It was in the hallway leading to it.'

Ophelia narrowed her eyes, said nothing.

'There's a gilded mirror halfway down? I thought I glimpsed something that wasn't supposed to be there.'

A moderate lie.

An elucidation that didn't quite measure up.

Because he'd been asking about the *library*.

Not the hallway.

Thankfully, Ophelia did not seem keen to press the issue.

'It's a large house,' she said. 'And bursting at the seams with unconventional architecture. The eyes, unused to the elaborate style, can often be deceptive. I've been living here for years, and my head will often play tricks.'

Jaison nodded. 'You're right, of course.'

'Think of being inside Oaklyn like wearing a new pair of prescription glasses. When you take them off, the world can appear askew. At least at first. Just takes a while to acclimatize.'

Again, he felt a wave of dissatisfaction. Ostensibly, Jaison was seeking an ally – one that could potentially illuminate some of the house's secrets.

But there would be no ally in Ophelia Taylor.

Glancing down at immaculate fingernails painted the same red as her lips, Ophelia said, 'For dinner, I've got Declan doing some prep work – he often helps me in the kitchen. But it's high time I joined him.'

Jaison glanced at his wrist, a habit from another lifetime. 'I guess it's time to explore some more,' he said.

'Keep following the path that brought you here. You'll discover some ponds teeming with Koi fish.'

'Thank you. I might do that. One thing … sometime today, I was hoping to meet Montha. Do you know where he'll be?'

Devoid of joy, Ophelia's normally placid features became doleful. 'Montha? Why would … well, he *does* spend a lot of time outdoors. So perhaps you'll meet him soon.'

'Let's hope.'

'Have a wonderful afternoon, Jaison. Perhaps we'll see you in the kitchen for supper tonight?'

With this, the chef stood. Soon her fashionable brogue shoes found purchase on the footpath.

Observing her depart, Jaison could only think of Selena.

Disappearing down the fireman's pole with the same hurried abandon.

***

Despite professing an interest, Jaison had no desire to discover ponds teeming with Koi fish.

He wanted to locate the chapel.

Amelia's sometime home.

Which entailed trudging north, away from the castle, occasionally using the giant monolith as a compass point.

After twenty minutes of negotiating verdure and flora to rival any botanical garden, his search finally yielded something.

First a hint of wood smoke; drifting grey cloud with the accompanying smell of ash. Then a needlepoint steeple, one whose apex hovered above a line of red oak trees.

Through foliage, Jaison spied white brick festooned with green moss and lichen.

Of a smaller scale than predicted, the chapel's design was evocative of thousands conceived and built during frontier times. Externally decrepit, there was no outward evidence the building presently served as a home.

Square windows with green glass veiled the interior.

A white door, arched and wooden, provided access.

Conscious somebody might be observing him from inside, Jaison stepped out of the trees and approached the first of two dozen stone steps.

On the precipice of knocking, he was suddenly overcome by a surfeit of images. His imagination, untethered, was providing details of a past he hadn't asked for.

In his mind's eye, he witnessed the spiritually and physically sick using this building for succor. Old men and women staggering up the steps to attain atonement and judgment in equal measure.

A group who had once used the castle as makeshift barracks, Jaison saw military personnel seeking guidance from a guru inside.

Because they were at war within themselves.

From underneath the door, Jaison smelled incense, sweet and somehow unpleasant.

Instead of knocking, he tried the knob.

It turned easily in his palm.

***

Inside, a small log fire burned.

Walls were garlanded with murals.

A hybrid of the religious and secular alike.

Red carpet covered space the size of a small apartment.

No pews adorned this room.

No candle festooned altar stood raised at the end.

Instead, there were sectional sofas in a u-shaped configuration and a large television unit.

Laden with used dishes and ashtrays, a coffee table completed the ensemble of a living room.

Paperback books peppered the carpet and couches with the disordered arrangement of a student's lair.

Absorbing the environment, he was at first oblivious to the walls.

And what hung from them.

Bloodied crucifixes.

Three affixed to his left, three to the right.

And hanging from each, a small figure.

Schooled in Christian mythology, Jaison assumed the emblems were orthodox in origin: that Christ dangled from each one. Yet it was apparent (as he moved toward the closest), these symbols were of a different order.

Crucified within a skein of dripping red was a string-wrapped skeleton.

Embedded filigrees of design pervaded the rood; the cross itself appeared metal.

The skeleton plastic.

Something of pagan derivation?

A Wiccan trinket of ritual.

Dark silver functioned as eyes.

Encircling the skull: bulbous teeth bereft of lips.

Embedded in the feet and palms, nails the size of picture hooks.

Blood saturated crosses, the forefront of

Jaison's awareness, had regulated the wall illustrations to the background.

Now he studied them, taking in a hodgepodge of paintings and word clouds.

A visual representation of the Garden of Eden took up two-thirds of the eastern wall. Naked and frolicking, Adam and Eve shared space with camels, horses, and tigers. In the foreground, a river churned. Close to the couple swayed a tree, one whose branches bristled with ring-tailed monkeys and various birds.

As well as a serpent.

Serpentine, Lucifer's body lay coiled around the trunk, his upper portion seemingly composed of the tree itself.

A wooden imp proffered Eve with lascivious intent.

Stains on the plaster and brushstrokes led Jaison to believe the painting was longstanding, perhaps commissioned only a short time after the chapel came into being.

Considerably cleaner, the west wall contained something different.

A stuffed doll within a five-point star.

Scrabble tiles and cutting implements orbited the doll. As well as hieroglyphs and herbs.

Their wicks alive and burning bright, rune-inscribed candles were positioned at the foot of this mosaic.

The gardener lives here. Lives in an old church fit for a modern witch. Does all this go in my book?

Wondering how such a chapter would read, Jaison suddenly heard a strong female voice speak from the entrance.

'In my right hand I hold some mace. In my left, a cell phone. Police are on speed dial. Tell me who you are, and I might not call them.'

As in the library, Jaison froze.

Caught in the act of doing something he shouldn't.

Before turning around, he raised both hands – an ingrained response.

A small woman with short brown hair stood on the steps.

Wearing dirt-stained overalls, her left hand indeed carried a phone. Not visible, her right was a bulge through a large pocket in the denim.

'Speak up,' said the woman.

Jaison tried to smile … but the attempt felt ill-conceived. Some instinct whispered any kindness on his part would be summarily dismissed in this standoff.

Then the woman's face slackened as comprehension dawned.

He said, 'I apologize for not knocking. To be honest, I'm not sure what I was thinking. I mean, Arabella *said* this was a converted apartment.'

'You're Jaison? The new guest?'

Jaison lowered his hands. 'And you must be Amelia?'

'Arabella informed you someone lives here. Did she *also* give you the freedom to just invade their personal space?'

With relief, Jaison observed Amelia's right hand retreat from her pocket – though a bulge remained.

'Honestly. I have no idea what I was thinking.'

Nor did he. Initially having the intention to knock, Jaison felt compelled to enter by something …

External.

A driving force whispering of strange taboos inside.

Behind his back, he saw Amelia's eyes change as those taboos became visible.

'It's not what you think,' she said.

Polite, Jaison was perfectly capable of telling a white lie when the situation demanded it. He said, 'I'm not one to leap to conclusions.'

But that's blood on those crosses – either animal or human. Which leads me to conclude you're a gardener who dabbles in some kind of weird magic.

Then, as if in affirmation, Amelia said, 'Hoodoo. Have you heard of it? Do you know what it is?'

Seeing her up close, Amelia's role at Oaklyn

became physically evident. Her hands, hidden until now, were dirt encrusted. On her forehead, sweat glistened.

Blue denim overalls were stained an emerald green.

Thinking of Selena's book, Jaison said, 'I've heard some things in passing, yes. Mainly from Hollywood. It's got nothing to do with traditional Voodoo, right?'

'That's right. It's a spiritual practice that combines elements of Christianity, even aspects of Islam. And its origins can be traced back to African slaves in North America.'

Amelia's words had the formula of a narrative, of something recited. They were, Jaison mused, words she'd previously used.

'Your personal proclivities, or in this case religion, are not my business.'

Visible relief coming over her face, the gardener sagged.

Gesturing with a green thumb, she encouraged them to step out of the building.

Outside again, Jaison became acutely aware of the chapel's oppressive interior; how every aspect had exuded a negative charge.

Spying a wheelbarrow containing potted saplings, he asked, 'How long have you been landscaping Oaklyn Castle?'

'Fifteen years. When I worked here for the

previous owner, I was part of a team.'

'There's nobody else to help you now?'

'Not exactly. My friend Eden …' Amelia trailed off, appeared to shrug the thought away. 'Boyd and Arabella are a different kind of employer. For them, it's all about privacy. So, Arabella's household staff is small.'

This statement piqued Jaison's interest. While Ophelia provided no insights, perhaps the gardener would be more forthcoming.

'There's Ophelia and Declan, and you. May I ask how many other staff live on the property? Are there other children here besides Vanita and Kingston?'

'This is something you need to know for the book?'

'Not really. This morning … I thought I saw a young person beside the pond. I have a view of it from my bedroom.'

'Then you probably saw Vanita.'

'That's the thing. It wasn't her. The child – I *think* it was a child – appeared male. He was wearing a dark green raincoat.'

Amelia's expression, somewhat scornful upon his first query, changed to misgiving. 'Years ago, during the winter, I sometimes brought my nephew here. But not anymore. As far as I know, Kingston and his sister are the only children. You say the child was wearing a raincoat?'

'Yes. Even with the distance I could see that.'

Amelia looked beyond him; her eyes glazed. 'That's strange. My Mark used to wear a slicker. I hardly saw him without it.'

'Mark …'

'My nephew. At first, he loved the house, loved coming here. And he loved the family even more. Then one day I guess he didn't.'

'He doesn't stay anymore?'

'No, he doesn't. On some weekends he'd get lost. Walking in the gardens. Nobody could find him anywhere. Sometimes he'd end up as far as Sagg Swamp.'

The name itself rang a bell.

A nature reserve, Jaison recalled. One that could be explored by bridges and walkways.

Glancing at the wheelbarrow, he said, 'The outside of the estate – it's as beautiful as the inside.'

Amelia considered this.

'You want to know how I manage it all? Eden, our maintenance man, also has a background in landscaping … and sometimes I'll work through the night.'

Out of politeness he wanted to query more in relation to her work – but Amelia could read his troubled expression.

'You're still thinking about those crosses, aren't you? I assure you, the work I do is benign.'

'I wasn't.'

'Yes, you were. And it's perfectly natural to wonder. Because Hoodoo is a greatly misunderstood tradition. It was my mother who taught me its beliefs – and I taught myself its practices. We have rituals, and we have spells. For anyone uninitiated, I think it's safe to assume these can appear creepy.'

'You practice a form of magic?'

'Hoodoo *is* magic. But it's neither black nor white. A practitioner will dictate whether it's used for liberation – or for bondage or ruin.'

It was an odd remark … and Jaison might have pressed for more.

But the skies chose that moment to open.

A few droplets at first, then a sustained pattering. Soon, the chapel's roof echoed to a rhythmic drumbeat.

'Thank you for stopping by today, Mr. Winters,' said Amelia, using the rain as an escape hatch. 'But I really should be getting back to it.'

Would Amelia continue her pottering outdoors? As likely as not, there were Boston ferns to attend inside the house. Vegetation every bit as deserving as the wonderland outside.

He said, 'Apologies about before. It wasn't my intention for us to get off on the wrong foot.'

By way of reply, Amelia returned to her wheelbarrow.

Before taking his own leave, Jaison cast a

sidelong view back at the chapel.

Once a shrine, now a tenement, there was no denying those moss-stained walls were still pervaded by an ecclesiastical aura.

Much like the castle.

An edifice whose grey stone had been transformed, by the onset of rain, into a gothic mirage.

***

After dinner, Arabella invited their new guest to watch a movie with the family in the main living area. Present for the occasion would be everyone.

Besides Amelia and Montha.

A once-a-week tradition, movie night had originally been Vanita's idea.

Shortly after Ophelia served popcorn, all the children came down from their rooms.

Tonight's viewing: a science-fiction romp starring Boyd Palmer.

For a few hours, Ghost Dad would be present.

Navigating the perils of space inside a television screen.

Kingston said, 'I don't see why we can't watch it in the cinema. What's the point of having one if we barely use it?'

'Because this is *intimate*,' replied Vanita, mouthing the words around popcorn. 'Besides, I *prefer* to watch it in here. The cinema is always so *noisy*. I sometimes feel like my eyeballs and ears are gonna explode.'

A private cinema within Oaklyn.

This was the first time Jaison had heard it mentioned.

Seeing his curious expression, Arabella said, 'It's on the basement level. And Kingston's right – we hardly ever use it.'

'Not true,' said Selena. 'Daddy likes to entertain his golfing buddies with movie marathons.'

'Yes, he does. You're welcome to use it anytime you wish, Jaison. You'll show it to him, won't you Declan?'

'No problem,' said Declan. 'I'll even show you how to work the projector booth. It's built like one of the old school boxes from the Forties. Boyd had it custom designed.'

'Really? Like you play films on celluloid?'

Declan chuckled. 'Nothing so romantic, I'm afraid. I just mean the physical design. There's a 35mm projector with a carbon-arc lamphouse, that sort of thing. But it won't run nitrate films. In a nutshell, it's a dummy. Basically, everything is automated. Programs are stored in digital format on a computer hard drive – and content is delivered over the Internet. Still, it's a sight for a cinephile's eyes.'

Ophelia, sitting next to Declan, seemed appalled at this.

'You consider yourself a *cinephile*? But you've admitted to skipping most of Arabella's films. What kind of movie buff *hasn't* seen every film Arabella Jaqus has made? She is the *queen* of modern cinema.'

A throw pillow was launched in Ophelia's general direction.

Beaming, Arabella said, 'Whatever I'm paying you, Ophelia … it simply isn't enough.'

'Whether that's true or not hardly matters,' said Declan. 'Arabella dabbles in certain genres, mainly drama. And this particular movie buff haunts a very *specific* cinema landscape.'

Ophelia chortled. 'Wait … are you saying you don't *like* drama films? That you don't watch them?'

'How do I put it? Drama films are … terrifying. Bloody scary, in fact. Give me a horror film over something the Academy jerks off to any day of the week. They're far less depressing and entirely fun.'

Selena covered both her ears. 'I didn't hear that. I didn't.'

'Declan,' Arabella scolded. 'Could you *please* refrain from lewd language when children are present? I hate to think what lecherous adjectives you use when I'm not around.'

'Nothing they haven't heard before in a

schoolyard,' Declan said. 'Or, I might add, from one of your films. Ophelia, could I have more butter for my popcorn, please?'

Her body language registering distaste, Ophelia moved a sitting position away. 'Is there something wrong with your legs? Get it yourself, you dumb ox.'

Observing the repartee, Jaison grinned.

Soon after, a giant flat screen roared to life, the Universal logo – and its accompanying music – acting as a prompt for the room to fall silent.

Then a handsome and smiling Boyd Palmer had everybody's full attention.

Armored in a spacesuit, Boyd began moralizing about human power surges, the solar system, and the ultimate end of all life on the planet. Thereafter, it fell to this fictionalized Boyd to go about the business of *saving* all life … and receiving personal redemption by doing so.

In the appropriate places, Kingston and Vanita cheered and clapped.

They were happy to see their father saving the day.

Despite their earlier skirmish, Declan and Ophelia inched closer to each other.

Whether their relationship was romantic or otherwise, Jaison perceived a deep, mutual respect.

While his encounters in Oaklyn Castle thus far had been disquieting, the writer could acknowledge

a certain contentment sharing space with Arabella's
extended family.

6

Before arriving at Oaklyn Castle, Declan Avery led a frenetic life peopled with artistic types: men and women who existed under the banners of writer and actor.

As a young man growing up in Missouri, he observed blue collar workers reap their share of local respect, his own family and friends paying him no dividends when Declan attained a B.A. in English Literature from Washington University in Saint Louis.

It was during this time (when his immediate peers were signing up for Dubya's sequel war in the Middle East) that Declan Avery made preparations to visit the river community of Hannibal, a town where the museum complex of Mark Twain's boyhood home resided. He hoped, by visiting, it would provide the impetus to kickstart his own writing career.

Or perhaps the locale would serve as a catalyst to pen the *Great American Novel*.

Though the epiphany never arrived, it was here

– not far from the Twain gift shop – where Declan met by chance a fellow wordsmith: Oliver Goldman.

A Hollywood wordsmith, no less.

Goldman (fortyish, greying, smart as a tack) was the critical darling behind three successful independent films. On that day browsing cheap Twain merchandise, a mentor-friendship formed. And thereafter, Oliver Goldman taught the young and budding writer the subtle art of penning screenplays.

The Great American Novel, while still a persistent ambition, would have to wait.

Because Declan had inadvertently discovered his true talent.

As if born to the medium, he churned out scripts … the kind of stories featuring washed-up boxers, courtroom antics, and family sagas. For a time, he'd also been proficient in science fiction. Presently in vogue were robotic law enforcement romps and time-travelling cyborgs.

Competence – as many in the Hollywood writing game could attest – did not guarantee success.

Declan devised an attack plan: spend seven years schmoozing the Hollywood elite and their inner social circles, hoping (at the very least) to have one of his screenplays adapted by a major studio. Though the stratagem was ill-conceived and slapdash, he moved from Missouri to the outskirts of Los Angeles shortly after his graduation.

But Declan's end goal for success did not go as planned.

Instead of becoming a revered writer of original prose, he somehow began a career polishing *other* people's scripts.

Essentially, Declan Avery became a ghost writer.

A thing the novelist within balked at.

Of all the advantages ghost writing can offer, Oliver Goldman imparted one day, *one of the greatest is that you get to meet interesting people.*

The day in question was at a party, and both men were drinking gin and tonic. Declan, on the cusp of protesting Oliver's philosophy, looked around at the party's assorted guests … and realized his friend was right.

Because interesting people – in this case, celebrities – were everywhere.

Some were minor. But wasn't that Alicia Silverstone helping herself to a tray of chicken? And near the bar – Declan swore he was staring at a morose-faced Spike Lee.

I might be a ghost writer – someone who hasn't broken through with their own stuff. But I'm in this room, aren't I? Sharing cocktails with movers and shakers.

It was a pivotal revelation and (much later)

turned out to be a crucial party.

One whose guest list included the formidable Arabella Jaqus.

At the time, Arabella had been up-and-coming – someone who was yet to meet Boyd Palmer; that particular rendezvous to occur two years later after they were coupled together in an assassin romp.

When a terrible male singer had taken to a makeshift stage, Declan and Arabella made each other's acquaintance.

Ostensibly to relieve his bladder – mainly wanting to escape the sounds issuing from the stage – Declan downed his gin and made a beeline for the men's room. Mere meters from the door, he'd collided with the movie star … who appeared on her own urgent mission to find solitude.

Adjusting her dress, she said, 'If you asked me what I prefer, the sound of vomiting or *this* – I'd have to go with the sound of vomiting.'

'He sounds like a dying cat,' Declan remarked.

In unison, they laughed.

Later, Declan would pinpoint this moment where their connection formed. He, the hack from Missouri. She, the bourgeoning actress.

An actress whose star burned so bright it eclipsed everyone else.

Locking eyes with Arabella, he perceived a deep honesty … in addition to a droll sense of humor similar to his own. And – though he couldn't be sure – he suspected she perceived something similar in him.

In the past, tabloid magazines went to great lengths to besmirch Arabella's name. Declan asserted – in that moment – the stories were concocted lies.

When the laughter died, Arabella asked, 'Have we met before?'

'I don't believe so.'

'You have the air of an extra.'

Declan tried to appear miffed.

'An extra? I guess that means lacking the mystique of a leading man?'

'I didn't mean –'

'Actually, I've never stood in front of a camera.'

'You're a writer, then?'

'Guilty as charged.'

'Well, that was my first guess, believe it or not. I was just tiptoeing around. Didn't want to –'

'Insult me?'

'Insult you.'

There was more laughter. Thereafter, Declan divulged that United Artists optioned two of his screenplays – and Columbia requested rewrites of a third. Over the course of a year, he garnered the reputation as someone *in the making*. A wunderkind biding his time until his *big break*.

'But I'm not holding my breath, of course,'

said Declan. 'If this gig doesn't pan out, I'll probably head back to Missouri. Get a teacher's certificate, maybe.'

For some reason, he had the movie star's full attention. With curious aplomb, she asked, 'What, pray tell, are you going to teach?'

'Literature. The only subject I ever knew anything about.'

Soon after, they took their drinks outside, and there followed discussion concerning all the greats Declan had spent a lifetime studying. Everything from *One Hundred Years of Solitude* to *Dracula*.

During their talk, Arabella discovered his love of children – despite not having any of his own. (Perhaps a reason he wanted to teach.) And she confided she desired her own.

And confessed she entertained the notion of adoption.

Bestowing the gift of a bright future to someone from an impoverished family had been close to her mother's heart.

And she'd seeded Arabella with the same ambition.

***

It was an unlikely friendship that survived the years and everything an uncertain world parceled out.

Such as Arabella's journey to superstardom.

And Declan's eventual failure as a Hollywood wordsmith.

No longer *in the making* – and barely requested as a ghost writer, either – he came to the growing realization his time among the Hollywood traps was nearing its end.

Was he bitter regarding this outcome?

Ultimately, he was not.

You took a shot at a difficult market – and almost made it. Twain once proclaimed there's no sadder thing than a young pessimist. So be proud of what you briefly achieved.

Throughout their time together, Declan bore misgivings that Arabella would abandon the relationship in the wake of his decision to return home.

Those fears proved unfounded when Arabella became pregnant with the offspring of Boyd Palmer.

'We've decided to make you the godfather,' she said one afternoon before his scheduled flight back. It was autumn, and Declan was looking forward to seeing hickory trees at the height of their fall display. 'Well, *I've* decided. Boyd didn't exactly have much of a say in the matter. But he trusts me implicitly. So, what this means is … you must come back here and visit me regularly. After all, the children will have to get to know you.'

'Children?'

'Oh, you haven't heard? I'm expecting twins. Lord, if some of the gossip rags have cottoned on to this fact – how is it that *you* remain unaware?'

Gape mouthed; Declan did not reply immediately. Not because of the revelation she and Boyd were expecting twins. No, it was her lackadaisical declaration he was going to be a godparent.

To powerful Hollywood children, no less.

While Arabella, in her formative years, absconded religion, the tradition still carried weight in her immediate circle. More than anything, the gesture seemed to be symbolic: a way to strengthen their relationship and establish a family bond.

Family.

The word itself felt nonsensical, somehow lacking substance. It was – for Declan Avery – a thing reserved for other people.

An only child shackled with parents who never hid their outward disdain of his craft, this alien notion of *family* was a concept that managed to simultaneously elicit feelings of fear and excitement.

Their energy, a fraternal one, Arabella was not – and never would be – Declan's lover. Yet by doing this she had gifted him with something even greater: a lifelong ticket to experience life together as a friend and confident.

'You'll at least think about it?' she'd asked.

But Declan did not *need* to think about it.

Shedding tears, he hugged his friend.

Only peripherally aware he was mumbling that wearing the title would make him proud.

***

True to his word, Declan returned home. Deciding to rent a cheap apartment in Richmond Heights, studious steps were then taken to obtain a degree in education.

With a Bachelor's degree to grease the wheels, Declan was able to take courses *and* instruct. After a year and a half – and the designated assessments passed – most of the hurdles to accreditation were cleared.

Most of them.

By far the largest obstacle was adapting to a normal life outside the neon haze of Los Angeles. Saturday nights, bereft expensive booze at lavish parties, now included a TV dinner and a single bottle of beer in front of the idiot box.

For the first few months in his new apartment, there was an undeniable freedom in these things … in addition to being away from his demanding laptop and having to inhale smog. Before long, however, ennui had settled in once again.

Missouri, while picturesque, could not compete

with a city of mesmeric females who looked like they belonged on the silver screen.

When Arabella finally called, Declan picked up the phone like a man on death row granted a last-minute reprieve.

Two summers prior Arabella had given birth; ongoing success and motherhood giving her cadence an undeniably optimistic edge.

'I know I haven't called as much as I should have,' she said. 'And that's totally on me. But I want you to know I think about you *all* the time. It's not an excuse but I've been extremely busy.'

Didn't Declan know it. Arabella Jaqus, star of the horror thriller *Bones of Men*, had recently been nominated for an Academy Award.

In addition to every other conceivable film accolade on the planet.

'Congratulations on everything – I truly mean it. When I tell some of the faculty you were one of my *besties*, almost no one believes me. That's to be expected, I guess. And I don't press the issue. Most of the academic types would turn their noses up if I *were* to be believed.'

'Why's that?'

'Well, according to these ideologues, anyone from Hollywood is basically a libtard.'

'That's actually what I wanted to talk to you about.'

'You wanted to talk about my faculty?'

'*No*, silly. I wanted to know if you're fully certified yet.'

'Oh, *that*. I'm not far off.'

Nor was he. With only two months of the teacher's program left, Declan's final barriers were a range of pedagogy and content-area assessments.

Initially, Declan sought one area of expertise – but he managed to go far beyond his first ambitions. Soon, he would be qualified to teach (in addition to literature), both humanities and English in secondary education.

With the sound of babies playing in the background, Arabella said, 'I'm excited to hear you say that. Relieved *and* excited. Boyd … he doesn't subscribe to my conviction in all things astrological. But I firmly believe the stars are finally lining up for us all.'

'Arabella … what *are* you talking about?'

'We've bought a place. But not just any old place. This will be a refuge from the world … a home where little Kingston and Vanita can thrive. It's on the East Coast – a castle big enough to raise a *horde* of children. And it's positively *dripping* with history and mystery. In fact, you've probably heard of it.'

A famous house on the East Coast. There were more than a few of those. But what quickly sprung to mind wasn't a house evincing mystery.

It was one steeped in blood.

The Amityville mansion.

Where Ronald DeFeo, Jr. butchered his family.

Later, the purported ghosts arrived.

Of course, his imagination was getting away from him. Arabella would never –

'It's called Oaklyn Castle,' she said, enunciating the title as though it contained a British inflection. 'Built on the North Shore of Long Island. You know, in those hills where every town is a hamlet? Get this, though. Oaklyn is an acronym that uses each part of the creator's name, reversed. Isn't that cool?'

Declan, who had no inkling of its history, agreed.

'It was built by a woman named Lyn Oak, with construction going on for about six years in the early 1900s. Can you imagine being a woman and building something so big? Especially back then? Anyway, we were told she came from German money – railroads, mainly. And aside from being a noted philanthropist, she was also a patron of the arts. Gosh, would you listen to me? I'm babbling. You know I always babble when I get excited.'

Familiar with the trait, Declan said nothing. He was thinking about Long Island – a stretch of real estate containing the DeFeo murder house, after all. While never setting foot outside the city during his travels to New York, that particular region was well known.

One could even say notorious.

And so was Oaklyn Castle.

Not as infamous as Graceland, of course. Or George Washington's estate out there in Virginia. But it held its own as recognizable. A building that had gone through numerous incarnations – including being abandoned for untold years – before eventually settling into the present century as a landmark where wealthy people got married and your average citizen wanted to drive past for an obligatory Facebook selfie.

That Arabella Jaqus and her husband were going to live there was somehow foreseeable.

And yet equally surprising.

'Of course I've heard of Oaklyn Castle. Who hasn't?'

Endeavoring to keep the surprise out of his voice was proving difficult.

Because Arabella's next words confirmed he was broadcasting it loud and clear.

'You're wondering why a Hollywood brat would even *consider* moving East, aren't you? And you're probably thinking back on all our conversations where I staunchly declared I'd *never* move. Pasadena bitch, born and bred. That's what I said. And the daughter of a Sunkist real estate mogul, no less. Not only is the business of *film* here, but so is Daddy and all his connections. Why would I pull up stakes and move to a hamlet?'

Declan realized that, without voicing a word of his own, Arabella had succinctly laid out his thoughts. Granted, he didn't know this woman as intimately as others … at least not on the same level as someone like Ophelia, for instance. Yet he knew enough to realize her chosen choice for a sea change was …

Somewhat perplexing.

After all, Arabella was an extrovert.

Someone who rigorously avoided solitude if it could be helped.

Which probably meant …

'I think I understand,' he said. 'It's almost a cliché, but having children changes everything, doesn't it? Like it rewires your brain. You're not thinking about you and Boyd, you're thinking of them. You want the twins to grow up in a world far away from soulless men and women. Do you also remember saying that? That Hollywood is creatively uninspired and basically runs on egomania? Lord knows I lived there long enough to work some of this out for myself.'

Arabella said, 'They'll pay you a thousand dollars for a kiss.'

'And fifty cents for your soul.'

The quote was from Marilyn Monroe. And somehow it felt entirely appropriate. Because Declan often wondered privately about Marilyn's fate. Perhaps if she'd found enough courage to escape Brentwood and the kingpins who surrounded her, the final reel in her personal story might have ended differently.

After a moment of companionable silence, Declan asked, 'So I guess this means I won't be making any return trips to LA LA Land? You're still going to be working, though, right? And Boyd? I can't imagine that's ever going to change.'

'Of course, it won't. At the very least, I'll be doing commercials. Next year, I'm going to be the face of Guerlain Parfumeur's new fragrance, if you can believe it. Not to mention a billion charity events. And you're right – no more trips to LA LA Land for you. Because I want you live with us and see to it my children are properly educated.'

'Wait … what?'

'You know I've always dabbled with the idea of my kids being home schooled. At least partially home schooled.'

'Yes. You've mentioned this a few times.'

'Well … before long, you'll be a certified teacher with teacher credentials.'

'What are you trying to say?'

'Declan, this is the whole reason why I called you today. Very soon, after the sale is properly finalized, I want you to begin packing your things.'

'What for?'

'To move in with us, silly. We want you to move into Oaklyn Castle.'

***

Move into Oaklyn Castle.

As an avowal, it felt about as whimsical as the singular word *family*. Surely Declan Avery, the failed script doctor, had not been invited by a starlet to live in a world-renowned house?

Such outlandish propositions were reserved for other people.

Attractive as the idea was, Declan initially protested its merits.

Confident in his burgeoning aptitude as an educator, there were still dozens of other candidates more qualified for the task. In addition, tutoring preschoolers; enlightening *children* was a type of schooling he'd given only cursory thought to.

Declan had to admit that Arabella's argument, while flawed, contained its own weird weight.

Wanting no outsiders living on the estate, she and Boyd desired someone they could trust unreservedly.

An alternative soul, Arabella Jaqus had always sought alternative modes of living. Not only had she applied unconventional methods nurturing her acting career, but she also adopted avant-garde techniques to every other aspect of her life.

Including and not limited to: health issues, fiscal matters, and intellectual pursuits.

When it came to helping her raise the twins –
and potentially other family members down the line
– was it really that surprising she would recruit
Declan Avery for the effort?

No – it's just like her.

Before acquiescing to the invite (and changing
the course of his life forever), there were certain
things he needed to shore up. Adding to his training
certificates for one … and reconciling in his mind
obligations inside the castle included being a
caregiver – if not an outright au pair – to genetically
matched children he had yet to meet.

While the first thing was easy to resolve, the
second would prove far more challenging.

Sleepless nights prevailed.

After a week, Declan called Arabella and
informed her of his decision.

Six months later, Long Island became his
permanent home.

***

Oaklyn Castle was haunted.

And discovering this did not happen overnight.

Much like a dam breaking, the process was
gradual.

First, a chipping away of the sediment –
sediment in this instance being a euphemism for
Declan's psyche – then a significant crack resulting

in a deluge.

Within his first year as a resident of Oaklyn Castle, Declan became convinced the house was riddled with ghosts.

But not haunted in a way anybody could easily imagine or comprehend.

Conventionally, spirits in old houses had their foundations underscored in a hundred supernatural movies. Largely, these phenomena involved things like unexplained noises (footsteps and voices) or household objects moving of their own accord. On occasion, people glimpsed beings who were corporeal in nature.

Ethereal figures and shapes assuming the form of dead people.

Oaklyn Castle had all these things.

And yet none of them.

Because the beating heart of what made the phenomena tick was not the environment itself.

Before Arabella and her growing brood entered, Declan had little doubt the house was ordinary.

Insofar as any of these ancient houses were.

Sure, they produced strange noises – and their architecture lent itself to the otherworldly.

But sometimes it took a group of people for a house to wake up.

Or in Oaklyn's case, a single person.

***

In the beginning, things fared well for Declan; his initiation into the new home exceeded expectations. Back then, Boyd Palmer was in regular attendance, overseeing the transfer of his family with an authoritarian, almost militaristic purpose. Until their first introduction, Boyd was nothing but a glossy face superimposed on magazines. A likeable macho man observed solely in big budget action films and historical dramas.

Movies that made everyone – including male audience attendees – swoon.

Before shaking his hand, Declan felt completely nervous – and rightfully so. Arabella's husband, an intimidating presence, was sizing up the man who would teach and pamper his children.

Luckily, it didn't take long for a bond to form.

Because both men desired to see a certain woman flourish.

And both were familiar with the artistic process of attempting to paint another world into being.

Equally nervous about meeting the children, Declan's fears were similarly unfounded. Playful and extroverted like their mother, Vanita and Kingston soon grew to adore the man who taught them reading basics.

They also came to cherish their time together building forts or simply being chased around the hallways of Oaklyn Castle as though it were an elaborate labyrinth.

The children grew into preadolescence. By the time they were ready to begin reading Mark Twain, their caregiver could hardly recall a time they weren't.

It was the house.

Making him believe time in the real world had somehow become irrelevant.

Their roles in the house cemented, Declan's relationship with the gardener became a cordial one. Beyond exchanging pleasantries, there was seldom a need to converse.

He'd known Ophelia Taylor in the outside world … but it was inside the mansion where their rapport truly flourished, subtle flirting becoming a hallmark of the connection. Once, after too many margaritas, Ophelia had taken him to bed.

But thereafter drew a line in the sand.

Our roles in Oaklyn are ultimately working ones, Declan. Further intimacies will strain the solidarity we've cultured.

While acquiescing (and agreeing) with the cook, Declan would always wonder what could have been.

Inexorably, Arabella and Boyd's long-held desire to adopt would bear fruit. After only two years, three teenagers with ebony skin had rooms of their own and were busy acclimatizing to a new life away from their original places of birth.

Whereas Selena, Phuoc, and Montha seemed affable enough, they were not Declan's sole focus of intent. Separate from the realm he was nurturing with the twins, Oaklyn's new additions fell under the umbrella of their mother's ministrations.

In the beginning, things fared well.

But then came the time shifts.

And the sound of sobbing within the walls.

***

Crying as a constant.

The laments of a boy and girl.

When hearing the sound, investigations only yielded the placid forms of sleeping twins. Further examinations led Declan to conclude no phones or televisions (or any other natural noises) accounted for what reached his ears.

Gentle sobs of torment.

Muffled tears of pain.

Sounds nobody else seemed to notice.

Briefly, he found the sound of crying almost comical.

Taking into consideration his present home.

The mournful wail of lost children? It's like Oaklyn Castle is suddenly the setting for one of Arabella's horror movies.

Almost comical.

But never genuinely so.

Because the tempo of crying wasn't average or something you got used to.

The tears were akin to weeping piped through the throat of a child near death.

As though whoever cried was recalling a vast cavalcade of human experiences, memories saturated with a nuance of misery not easily catalogued or defined.

Declan's attempts to record the phenomena were often met with failure.

On a rare occasion he managed to record *something* of import, what came through his speakers wasn't the sound of weeping.

Instead, the phone yielded a type of elegy one might hear in a church.

The whispered entreaties of a singular worshipper.

One whose deity existed in direct opposition to a loving God.

Often, he contemplated sharing his dilemma.

If not with Arabella herself, then surely Ophelia would be willing to lend an attentive ear?

Would Ophelia listen without shrugging off the spooky stuff as casual entertainment?

Ominous crying through the walls – Declan imagined Ophelia latching onto the subject matter as great fodder for late-night conversation.

Idle gossip while drinking exorbitantly priced bottles of *Torbreck Shiraz*.

Knowing her predilection for tarot cards and mediums, the cook would potentially enlist the help of outside forces.

Perhaps a clairvoyant.

A possibility which frightened him.

After weeks of contemplation, Declan decided to uncover – with the aid of Oaklyn's vast library – information to help his cause.

***

Inside the library, the first time-shift occurred.

Deprived of reaching the floor with his desired materials, Declan was traversing the spiral staircase when reality itself transformed.

Alone one moment, the ground floor abruptly came alive with a crowd of people.

Men and women ... even a few children.

Busying the aisles and chatting in hushed tones germane to libraries everywhere.

Though acutely aware of *them*, they seemed oblivious of the man on the staircase.

Give or take twenty people, many of them outfitted in the clothes of a warmer season: stonewashed blue jeans, fitted shirts, and halter tops.

Some sported tartan flannel.

Solely used to a singular family using this space, observing a group of people that could be construed as the *general public* caused Declan to momentarily lose his footing.

Slipping, he just managed to keep a precarious hold on a balustrade, enough to keep him afloat.

Close by, a woman with blonde hair stood perusing books.

Intent on getting a closer look, Declan made his way down the staircase …

Before the world shifted again.

In lieu of the presence of live humans, the library became besieged with mannequins.

Dozens of them.

Some of the dummies were clothed.

But many weren't.

Flanking Declan's right, a vintage dummy with cracked and peeling skin stared upward at nothing.

Its eyes were elongated globs of grey.

Its bald pate was like a scarified globe.

Tendril fingers glossed in crusted nail polish reached toward Declan like hooked claws.

Behind a library desk, a male mannequin dressed in a suit brooded over reading material, his cane held crosswise over protruding knees.

Close to the entrance, two unclothed females were arranged in coitus, their position suggestive of sixty-nine.

Despite the manifestation being shocking – an event beyond phantom weeping – Declan retained enough basic faculties to apprehend what he was seeing.

Owen Headly's pet mannequin project.

This must have been what it was like, right down to a smell of tobacco in the air.

And the previous time shift …

Declan had gone back to a time when the castle operated as a hotel.

Not possessing the wherewithal to move, he caught the briefest glimpse of the second floor before the world returned to the present.

Enough time for him to discern even more mannequins, their poses numerous and their costumes ostentatious.

On that day, he discovered nothing in the library to help his cause.

*****

Striking at random, like instances of lightning, more time shifts followed in the proceeding months.

Once, alone in the movie theater while watching a horror film, Declan was interrupted by a guest in the back row.

A bald man.

Becoming adept at judging time periods, he placed the man's existence during the previous century. While the black suit he wore was standard – wide-peak lapels and two vents – his pale flesh and bald head were not.

Nor his gold-flecked eyes.

Eyes that regarded Declan with concealed mirth.

Never during a previous time shift had Oaklyn's occupiers been conscious of Declan Avery.

And never had there been attempts to communicate or connect.

Until now.

Seated in the furthest corner of the theater, the bald man tapped one elongated finger on the headrest in front.

There was no denying this stranger's inhuman nature.

In both clothes and charisma, he bore more than a passing resemblance to everybody's favorite vampire *Nosferatu*.

With the bold strains of a horror score filling the auditorium, rooted to his own seat, Declan wondered if this past specter was a specter at all.

Conceivably, the vampiric man was one of Ophelia's invited guests – present as an audience member and dressed for the show. Though outside visitors were seldom, it was still viable to bump into them on the odd occasion.

The previous night, Declan announced his intention to view the horror film.

An overt invitation for company.

As expected, nobody showed up.

Nobody except this guy.

A closer appraisal put the visitor notion to shame.

In addition to gold-flecked irises, the stranger's skin presented further foibles.

A face almost translucent, see-through, a liquefied mass of fluids seething beneath the skin.

Cognizant of Declan's realization, the man grinned.

Exposing grey incisors slicked with spittle, their points circuitous like a serpent.

Regrettably, an exit strategy meant circumnavigating this stranger.

Knowing this, Declan leaped from his seat anyway and bolted through the aisle like a man on a mission.

On the screen behind, a final girl began howling, her escape imminent through dark and treacherous woods.

***

Precisely when had Declan noticed something wrong with Montha?

He didn't know, exactly. Like everything else in the mansion, events progressed slowly. Montha, a regular presence walking hallways in the early days, decided at some stage to haunt the outside world instead.

Haunt.

Now there was a face that seemed to define the word. Perpetually sorrowful and withdrawn, the boy's eyes were like reflected oil.

One day, the young man from Haiti appeared an optimistic soul; someone who regarded his new life in America and Oaklyn Castle as a windfall. The next, he began to extricate himself from the family both physically and emotionally.

Up at dawn, Montha would spend an entire day outdoors, secret endeavors taking him well into the night.

Slowly, Declan began to understand something fundamental and frightening about his time spent on the grounds of Oaklyn.

The boy was building something.

And now (over a year later), this was the one truth Declan had retained.

Montha is building something.

Exactly *what* had been occluded by a kind of forced amnesia.

Whatever thing the boy was creating, Declan suspected he – at one time – accidentally stumbled across it.

Now, as a form of punishment, he could no longer leave the castle and return outside.

Of all the weird things to have transpired thus far (the endless sobbing, the shifts to different decades), somehow being forbidden from stepping outside remained the most astonishing thing of all.

Endeavoring to leave via the front door left Declan feeling dizzy and nauseous.

Brazen efforts to escape via side doors would end in periods of unconsciousness.

In the aftermath of one of these spells, he would often awaken in another part of the house.

On one occasion, he opened his eyes to find himself in the underground wine dungeons.

Having taken a battering in the wake of unexplained phenomena, Declan felt his sanity fraying to the point of imminent collapse.

***

With perils looming, Declan consoled himself by leaving windows of opportunity open for some kind of resolution.

Outside help – increasingly frowned upon by Arabella and Boyd – could surely be called upon.

There were old friends like Goldman, for instance. A man who would call in the cavalry should Declan profess he feared for his safety.

Another alternative was law enforcement.

Or simply sitting down with his oldest friend Arabella and unloading.

And say what? That I'm at the mercy of a supernatural maelstrom, and I suspect her adopted son is somehow pulling the strings?

Absurd.

Besides, he wasn't entirely sure the manor's mistress was entirely blameless.

Wasn't pulling strings of her own.

Progressively, Arabella exhibited a strong allegiance not solely to her children, but to the house itself.

As though it were a living entity.

Concluding his salvation lay in outside assistance only, all Declan had to do was pick up the phone.

His first efforts were rewarded with static.

And even stranger sounds.

The snarls and snorting of a creature: a Tasmanian devil, perhaps. A marsupial whose growls he'd become familiar with as a child.

But that descriptor wasn't quite apt, either.

Because whatever grunted and exhaled through the phone also had human qualities.

Placing a call to his mother, Declan was answered on this occasion by the sound of sobbing children.

As if his phone were scorching to the touch, Declan launched it across his room where it shattered into three separate pieces.

***

During his first months, Declan was surprised

at the lack of security. In Oaklyn, there were no guards present; no in-house offices crewed by a team of professionals to oversee the husband-and-wife movie stars. While this might be unusual in the modern age of stalkers and psychopaths, it wasn't entirely unheard of.

Especially for stars who chose to live on the outskirts of society, nestled away in fertile farmlands a short distance from sandy beaches.

Beyond the gates at night, a single hired security car performed a casual sweep of Oaklyn's anterior. They were a minor company, Declan knew – a service patrol whose main concerns during any given night entailed things like vandalism and break-ins. More for show than anything else, really.

No help is coming from the outside.

On some days with nothing but time on his hands, Declan began to think of alternative solutions.

Began to foment the kind of strategy one of his film heroines might concoct.

Something cunning.

Something left of field.

***

In the end, it was Ophelia Taylor who provided inspiration.

Ghost writer, she often called him.

A moniker applied when they were about the business of teasing each other.

Yes, once upon a time Declan worked as a ghost writer.

And there were, in essence, many others out there who were also skilled in the art.

Arabella herself voiced her desire to eventually appoint one to pen her own personal story.

A wordsmith of biopics and biographies.

Declan knew such a man.

Knew his reputation.

A writer who also haunted the Hollywood traps on occasion.

With gentle persuasion, Declan coaxed Arabella into reading the man's novels about other celebrities, many of whom were musicians.

Over time, she became enamored by the prose of Jaison Winters.

Delighted in his ability to adhere to the veracity of character.

With Arabella sold, Jaison became the perfect candidate.

Not for her biography, of course.

The perfect candidate for Declan Avery's rescue.

Since his first brush with the supernatural, he often marveled at his acting abilities – skills he developed among Hollywood phonies.

Aside from Montha, no one suspected he was

pulling strings of his own.

How are things going for you, Jaison? Have the time shifts started yet? Did you see anything in the library? From your demeanor, I suspect you did.

Soon a day would come when Declan posed these questions.

Until then, he continued playing his role as caregiver.

Because it was only a matter of time before a bald man with gold flecked eyes wanted to meet again.

7

Eleven days after arriving at Oaklyn Castle, Jaison encountered his first set of random stairs. Ominous and unforeseen, they emerged out of the morning fog like something marooned.

A beached shipwreck in the initial stages of succumbing to the elements.

Stairs leading to nowhere.

Today's early stroll had nothing to do with exploration or discovery – Jaison merely desired to get some exercise before beginning a writing session.

A staircase with nothing else attached.

Having solid sides, these particular stairs appeared composed of bluish-grey stone.

Steep and angular, they rose to a height of at least sixty feet, their apex clouded in a shroud of fog.

Tendrils of moss, indicative of age, grew on the sides like patina on rusted coins.

Approaching the steps head on, Jaison spied a humanoid figure balanced at the top.

His first thought
(the hooded midget has returned)
was waylaid by noticing this person had a well-proportioned physique.

Even through a skein of fog, he could discern dark skin.

Despite never meeting face to face, there were enough family portraits inside Oaklyn for him to conclude this was Arabella's orphan in the flesh.

Eager in the past to meet the teenager, Jaison felt less than enthusiastic about greeting him now. What he wanted (above all else) was to go back in time and undo his decision to leave the house.

The random stairs perturbed him.

And the appearance of Montha on the steps distressed him more.

'Mr. Winters,' came Montha's voice from his precipice. 'Have you ever seen stairs like this before? Have you, in all your wanderings, stumbled across an indiscriminate set of steps seemingly leading to nowhere?'

Raising his voice slightly to cover the distance, Jaison replied, 'I don't think I have; although, I remember reading about the phenomenon somewhere.'

In anticipation of his answer to the question, Montha's profile rocked back and forth, a gesture of acknowledgement.

He said, 'Since the rise of social media I've

seen them coming into the mainstream, people online bringing attention to the spooky appeal of random stairs. They say if you ever encounter stairs in a forest, you should never climb them under any circumstances.'

'Because …?'

'Because who knows where they'll take you.'

A short distance from the stairs now, Jaison was reminded of the steps leading up to the chapel – stone abutments weathered by time.

'But they're just ruins, right? Relics in the woods? Someone's old homestead or cabin?'

By degrees, the boy had edged closer to the ground.

'Occasionally, that's true. Yet they'll often appear in national parks, places no man has ever lived. Did you know that in the Namib Desert, Namibia, they once discovered a cast-iron spiral, the type of staircase one would usually encounter in a lighthouse … or Oaklyn Castle's library.'

He'd been on the verge of another question of his own – perhaps enquiring how they had managed to avoid each other until now.

But was hindered into silence.

For the briefest second, he was back in the library.

Reliving the moment.

Slamming the door on a suited stranger from the past.

Montha appeared to take visible delight in his discomfort.

'You must have spent some time in there, yes? Did you meet my sweet sister? You did, didn't you? Such a little stalwart, our young Selena. Always wanting to make the best of every situation. She's happy here, did she tell you that? She was happy to be kidnapped from her home in Cuba.'

With a single sentence, Montha was opening a hornet's nest of controversy: the kind of polemic debate he wanted to avoid.

Attempting to change the subject, he asked, 'So where did *these* stairs come from? Were they originally attached to anything?'

As though surprised to find the steps beneath him, Montha blinked. With delicate steps, one hand stroking the concrete support, he shuffled even further down.

'Yes.'

'Yes, they were attached to something?'

'Yes, to the question you *didn't* ask. What you didn't ask was have they always been here? Are they as old as the house itself? And the answer to that is *yes*. I discovered them during my first week here. These ones, at least. There are others.'

'Other random stairs?'

'The others …. you could say I'm their architect. Never eat soggy waffles.'

'What does *that* mean?'

Montha grinned. 'It's an old mnemonic we used back in Haiti, a way to recall the cardinal directions of north, east, south, and west. Never eat soggy waffles.'

'You're telling me there are other stairs located in each direction?'

Despite the pointless purpose of the stairs, Montha seemed impressed Jaison understood.

'Yes. There are others in accordance with governing laws.'

Jaison said nothing.

He had no idea what the boy alluded to.

'Tell me, Mr. Winters, how is your new novel coming along? While I do apologize for not making myself available, I cannot say I endorse my mother's decision to bring you here. Truth be told, I wasn't *aware* of her decision until recently.'

So many things to unpack.

The boy declared to be the architect of additional stairs, removing the impression they were in any way random.

And then he admitted to being unaware of Jaison's imminent arrival.

Perplexing enough, these things were made more confusing by an accent containing a veritable stew of different influences. There was native Haitian … but underlying this, Jaison also perceived an undercurrent of something elusive.

For a moment he studied Montha, observed his

muscle shirt and sandals.

He said, 'My new novel about your family's life here is coming along well.'

'Quite the atmosphere to get a book done, I would think. Not at all what you're used to back home. And trying to write sober these days, no less. How's that working out for you?'

His first instinct (to go on the defensive) was undermined by more pressing concerns.

Had Montha also been digging into his background?

Or was something stranger at play?

Back in the day, Jaison Winters participated in a slew of interviews detailing his ongoing struggle with alcohol – and most of them were available to anyone with Internet access.

And yet I can't imagine the boy doing that.

'Couldn't have been easy for you,' Montha went on. 'Going from cheap wine in the morning to nothing at all. Oh wait … it wasn't *always* cheap wine, was it? Sometimes you liked to drink mouthwash when nothing else was available. Which is never a good look, is it? I mean, I used to see that kind of desperation on the streets of Haiti.'

The morning was cold, but Jaison felt his cheeks burning.

Being dissected by Arabella on his first night was one thing – but having to undergo a trial of slights by someone so young felt insufferable.

Which led him to recall one of his first conversations with Declan while being shown to his room – how the caregiver alluded to Montha being an individual ill-at-ease in their environment.

A teenager who acted out.

But how is it acting out when they're telling the truth? Because the drunkard Jaison Winters did all those things ...

Some of this must have registered on his expression – because Montha's grin grew as he came down the final steps. Closer now, the boy's eyes were visible as bloodshot gashes; sweat beaded to his forehead like dew.

Jaison said, 'You seem to know a lot about me. And that's okay. Because I've made no bones about my battles in the past. Lots of people know about you and your family, too. In fact, most of the *world* knows. I honestly can't imagine what that's like.'

'You think you know *me*, Mr. Winters?'

'I saw pictures of you everywhere when you first came to the country.'

Exposing white teeth and light pink gums, Montha chuckled.

'You're referring to tabloid pictures my mother sold? Now I'm beginning to ask myself why she chose to employ you. How is it a writer decides a *photograph* makes up the measure of a man?'

For the second time, he felt himself blush.

Because the boy (despite his juvenile tone)

called him out again with a weird form of veracity.

How the hell has it come to this? How did I get into a heated exchange with Arabella's adopted child?

Now it made sense why Montha evaded him – was not present during family meals or movie nights.

Hostile, the boy's temperament lay visible in every runnel of perspiration.

In lieu of answering Montha's question, Jaison remained taciturn.

Hoping the young man would take his silence as waving a white flag.

But Montha was not swayed.

'Those vultures out there,' he said, and waved a forlorn hand toward the front gates. 'Know nothing about me. And nobody else in America possibly could, either. Not my mother. And certainly *not* my simpering and drowning father. The Western world, Mr. Winters, has failed in every aspect to comprehend the ideologies of others besides their own. How can they … when *their* ideologies are ill-formed?'

A rhetorical demand, again Jaison declined to answer.

'Did you know there are a colonized people in the east of Nigeria, the Igbos, who have always struggled to fathom the notion of *banking*. How, they reason, can any adult in their right mind hand over possessions for others to keep for them?'

Since the beginning of their dialogue, question upon question had been leveled. For now, Jaison endured the spiel, confident Arabella's son would find some catharsis in it.

And soon leave him alone to wander back to the mansion.

'For some reason, people have come to accept the only metric for modernity is through a Western lens … and this is the heart of the problem. My home country, once proud, was settled by an empire who ultimately misunderstood Haiti. In the end, the French were so thorough and debased in their colonialism, my nation was essentially hollowed out.'

Some distance from the castle, Jaison could discern the roof through a talus of trees. He said, 'You don't like your environment? You're not happy here?'

'Whether I'm happy or not is irrelevant. Because I'm presently bound here, Mr. Winters. That means I'm forbidden to leave.'

Forbidden to leave?

'Many young people in your position might feel differently. They might be grateful to be placed in Arabella's care. A wealthy woman with every resource –'

Cat quick, Montha was upon him before he had time to blink.

'Don't patronize me! Do you take me for ignorant, Mr. Winters? Someone who *isn't* aware of my mother's standing? Trust me, I'm intimately mindful of her and Boyd's status and personal motivations for everything they do. *Including* why they decided to adopt three children from parts of the world they deemed impoverished.'

Shoulders heaving, body language reflecting rage, Jaison comprehended Montha had been on the verge of striking him.

Holding his ground instead of shrinking back (though inwardly fearful), Jaison managed to keep his gaze level with the boy's.

Just as swiftly as the rage arrived, Montha appeared to grasp his loss of control.

Stepping back, he said, 'I'm sorry. It would seem I've caught the restlessness of cabin fever. The castle can do that to you – despite its sheer size. Anxiety and anger … none of us here are completely immune to it. Paranoia, too, if I'm to be honest. Sometimes I see things that can't possibly be there. Is that something you've experienced of late, Mr. Winters? Paranoid delusions? Or even … paranoid illusions?'

He's playing with me, Jaison realized. *Having fun like a cat with prey.*

On the heels of this thought was a knowing apprehension Montha was fully aware of his brushes with the supernatural.

'Are you asking me if I've encountered one of the suicide brides?' he said and laughed. 'I cannot say that I have. No phantom lesbians to report in my room or any other.'

'You're referring to one of my mother's pathetic stories? The tales she peddles to new guests? Such trite fables *those* are, cribbed from the mouths of previous owners like a crude game of Chinese whispers. No, what I'm interested in is *your* illusions. The phantasms raised from your past. With each individual here, things work differently. I mean, God knows someone like Ophelia is practically immune. But for an old drunk like yourself? I cannot begin to imagine the chicanery at play.'

'For the life of me I don't know what you're going on about, Montha. Are you trying to tell me in some cryptic fashion this house really *is* haunted?'

Those black, unwavering eyes.

Jaison didn't need to answer Montha's original question.

Because Montha could see the answer in *his* eyes.

Having endeavored to wear something like a poker face during their entire conversation, he could see the gambit had been ineffectual.

The boy knew he was lying.

I need to get away from him, he thought.

And began taking tentative steps to achieve this.

Oaklyn Castle presently felt as distant as a phantom moon.

Montha said, 'There's no help coming for you, Mr. Winters. No help for Declan or for any of us. Speaking of Momma's caregiver. Did you know he's trapped here? What he fails to understand is we're *all* trapped here … all just cogs in the god-awful machine. And I'm the salvation that can liberate us. So, go. Leave. Go back to your precious notes and try to make sense of what I am.'

Montha might have said more. Strange words like *conduit* and *amplifier* peppered in a lecture about not being accountable for what happened.

But he could not make sense of it.

His back turned, Jaison's walk built to a trot, arms pinwheeling in concert with a flustered stride.

I'm showing weakness.

Backing away from a boy who exhibited malevolence.

His few friends in the outside world would surely view this escape as craven.

Uncharacteristic for the writer who built his reputation on being outspoken and occasionally bullheaded.

Among trees again, his anxiety was exacerbated by being unable to recognize any path he'd earlier navigated.

Briefly, between a tall stand of cypresses, he was convinced Amelia's chapel loomed, its outer façade dirty like a wavering mirage.

That couldn't be right, could it?

He was on the *west* side of the castle.

Nowhere near the gardener's quarters or pissing cherubs.

Shortly after, Jaison came across the hooded midget again.

Like before, he immediately considered one of the twins.

Not them.

Because the face concealed inside the cowl of olive green looked ancient.

A wrinkled monstrosity wearing the body of a child.

Eyeing Jaison through a copse of fog-slicked ferns, his jacket like jungle camouflage, the midget lifted one arm.

Indicating the removal of his hood was imminent.

He wants me to see what lies beneath.

Before this could happen, Jaison turned right.

And began *sprinting* toward the general direction of the mansion.

Certain his search would be fruitless, and hours would be spent probing for familiar turrets, Jaison let out a sigh of relief when grey stonework suddenly bled into existence.

Oaklyn Castle might be medieval … but he had never felt more comforted by the sight of something so old.

<u>8</u>

<u>Notes: The Authorized Biography of Arabella
Jaqus.</u>

    *Much has transpired since last adding to these
notes.*
    But I feel like nothing has.
    How many days have I been here?
    Fifteen, or thereabouts.
    I cannot be certain.
    *At first, ignoring my cell was done purely for
pleasure: a spit in the eye of the despair it offers up
each day. Now I ignore it because there is little
reception and only at certain times of the day.*
    *Much like electricity is parceled out and
rationed in a country that must preserve it.*
    *Most days I awaken with only a rudimentary
sense of time.*
    *And though I don't like to admit it, I find this
aspect of my stay liberating.*
    *Because we all dream (perhaps
subconsciously) of a world devoid of time.*

Where every day is nameless and more: immortal.

Certainly, this is how Arabella and her family live, at least from what I've observed. And it's strange when I think back to how I previously envisioned her world – a woman held prisoner by a hectic schedule of phone calls and auditions – I almost laugh.

Granted, she presently remains between jobs.

And I'm told her obligations outside these walls are few for the moment.

But I never anticipated the castle to have a casual, almost holiday air.

What did Declan say on my first day?

'We're like one of those isolated tribes in the Amazon rainforest.'

With this, the caregiver was telling the truth.

While there's more to say about Arabella and Declan, my thoughts now linger on two other residents – the final pieces in Oaklyn's puzzle.

Montha and Amelia.

People who don't feel like people at all.

And what does this mean?

Amelia herself seems facile; a woman who looks normal but has all the superficiality of a character on a movie screen. Of course, I do realize her years living in semi-isolation can account for this. Sequestered here, she's forgotten how the human herd walk and talk.

The gardener's segregation would also explain her immersion into Hoodoo arts.

Even now, writing this, I shudder when thinking of her trinkets – those blood-soaked crosses possessing all the aesthetics of witchcraft in a bygone and bloodied era.

Her charms appeared malign, yes.

But I still came away with the impression she was somehow protecting herself.

From someone in the house.

Which leads inexorably to Montha.

The Haitian enigma who can be found scaling random stairs leading to nowhere.

Endeavoring to paint the boy in simple words leaves me feeling bereft. For I struggle to articulate the sheer strangeness and hostility stemming from the nineteen-year-old. If I had to make a haphazard guess, I would say Amelia is trying to protect herself from him.

Which sounds more than absurd.

It sounds insane.

But is the notion any stranger than random stairs surrounding the property or a boy who claims to be their architect?

Is it any crazier than a hooded midget who prowls the outdoor realm like a ghost, his sole function seemingly to unnerve anybody who happens to cross his path?

Or a mirror man on the precipice of a self-

inflicted gunshot?

Yesterday, I sought to converse with Arabella about Montha. Of course, I wouldn't just blurt out some of my fears and misgivings regarding the boy; in my reputable way, I would approach things casually – even subtly.

On what floor does the boy sleep?

Does he ever take meals with his brothers and sisters?

Why did Ophelia cringe at the mention of his name?

But Arabella was nowhere to be found.

Not in the hallways, nor the kitchens.

Not even on her private number.

For two days, everyone seems to have vanished.

Except for Ophelia, who I briefly observed standing near the pond.

In what was once the ballroom, Declan was doing something that entailed soft music. Though I was of a mind to join him, his time spent in that part of the house feels like a private affair.

Taking the stairs back to my room, it momentarily occurred to me that perhaps no one is here.

Has never been here.

All this time, since the first hours after being dropped off by Arabella's escort, I've been interacting with nothing but air.

To quote Montha, paranoid illusions.

Distressingly, these thoughts did not abate, and I've found myself wondering if Oaklyn was empty and had conceivably fallen into disrepair.

As derelict and abandoned as during the years it was owned by a man who occupied it with mannequins.

I pictured myself sitting in a graveyard kitchen, sharing a meal with people I only imagined to be there.

I saw myself sitting on a decomposing sofa and watching a blank television screen with no one else.

Arabella's household – a family of ghosts.

Or I had imagined everything.

Madcap thoughts given life and strengthened by my own bourgeoning isolation.

In the aftermath of these fantasies, I spent some time online.

Making sure Arabella and her children were real people whose present address was a gargantuan castle on the East Coast.

Even more troubling than any of this ... my thoughts sometimes turn to having a drink.

Speaking of ...

How on earth did Montha know the true extent of my addictions?

In the movies, only devils and demons have access to that kind of baggage inside a person's skull. Invariably, they use such knowledge to torture a person into compliance.

Am I now entertaining the concept Montha is a demon?

While these notes exist for my own scrutiny, to be picked apart later, anybody reading this must be wondering on the progress of my novel.

Without the usual order applied to previous projects, haphazard pages have been strung together with no linear chapters.

I find the propensity to shower Arabella Jaqus with praise is a hard habit to break.

Because we've been conditioned, you see. Hardened by a multimedia brainwashing machine to view her in the unspoiled light of celebrity. In past novels, I've always attempted to tell the truth; however, getting to the root of Arabella's true essence will require a type of editorial prowess I ultimately feel ill-equipped for.

Would any writer be up to the task, though?

Taking into consideration all I have seen.

For some reason my thoughts keep returning to Amelia's bloodied talismans. They serve as a visceral reminder that Vanita passed on one of her own to me ... feels like a hundred years ago now.

The blue glass of her Nazar Boncuk.

So far, it has failed to protect me.

<u>9</u>

With so much of the house still left to explore, Jaison decided to visit Oaklyn Castle's indoor swimming pool.

From pictures, his mind recalled a coliseum-like environment of mosaic tiling evoking opulent Roman baths.

Stepping inside, he discovered a body of water even more elaborate than the realm depicted in portraits.

Like the bathhouses of old, a marine monster theme was chiseled into the mosaics.

Seashell chandeliers ornamented the ceiling.

Eight statues of Roman gods adorned the border.

He also spied an exercise room, sauna, and taped lines marking a handball court.

Earlier, before leaving his bedroom, he did not entertain thoughts of swimming; desired solely to look upon the shimmering blue and gold world seen in pictures.

Should have brought shorts and a towel ...

From the surface, a faint shimmer of condensation arose. As in a tepidarium, Jaison knew the water was heated.

Inhaling chlorine, he began circumnavigating the coping.

Toward the rear was a grid of windows – skylights powdered with painted stars.

Ornaments themselves, the walls were glass tiles of fused gold.

Additional Roman gods fronted the sauna like sentinels.

The slap of his footfalls strangely amplified, Jaison came to an abrupt stop.

Regarded the environment with new eyes.

Nothing had changed.

But something felt off-kilter.

Almost harmful.

At first, the feeling remained elusive.

Like the statues conspired against him.

Then he recognized the feeling.

Knowing you weren't alone.

Surveying things provided no immediate insight.

Everything close – the water, the cement, the gridded windows – appeared just as they had when Jaison first entered.

Yet the emotion of being watched was unmistakable.

Somewhere close to the first statues came the

slap of water being disturbed.

Then a splash.

His conscious mind reconciled to meeting something monstrous, Jaison turned around.

To be greeted by Phuoc.

Wading into the water with a plastic bag attached to his back.

'You didn't see me before, did you?' said Phuoc. 'You thought you were alone?'

'Where were you?'

The boy pointed to a group of benches on his left. 'Over there.'

'Why didn't you say hello? Announce yourself?'

Beginning to tread water, the boy only shrugged.

Frustration trickled into Jaison's awareness.

These children are a riddle.

And their strange way of communicating made him feel more at odds with the environment.

Self-conscious of an audience, Jaison decided to forego an inspection of the rear.

In lieu of this, he rolled up his trousers and removed his shoes and socks.

Sitting down, he lowered his feet into the water.

Oblivious, Phuoc began swimming.

Observing him, Jaison noted the boy's freestyle was awkward, the attached bag he wore like a bulging tumor.

Phuoc stopped, proceeded to grip a portion of coping on the opposite side. Turning around, he regarded Jaison with a blank stare.

'How deep is the pool?' Jaison asked.

'Five feet at the deep end, I think. You're not swimming?'

'Forgot my trunks.'

Phuoc's eyes narrowed.

'Swimming shorts,' he explained. 'What we called them as kids. Why do you have a bag on your back?'

Rubbing makeshift shoulder straps, Phuoc said, 'Growing up, we used to have these big waterfalls near my village. Whenever we went swimming, my real mom would make me wear one of these.'

'As a life jacket, I suppose. I guess it works?'

'It works. The waterfall pools used to be a great place to swim. That was before all the tourists came.'

'I've never actually travelled to Vietnam. Only parts of Thailand. One of my friends lives there and her online photos are amazing.'

This time in concern, Phuoc creased his eyes again.

'I wouldn't call it amazing. Before my natural parents died, we lived in a big building that used to house American soldiers. The building had thirteen floors. My neighbor lady told me that's why so many bad things happened there.'

'Because there were thirteen floors?'

'Yes.'

I've done it again, Jaison thought. *Brought up a sensitive topic I have no business asking about.*

Coupled with the ineptness, there was an undeniable curiosity.

The boy had secrets he appeared willing to give up.

'Superstition can be powerful. You said some bad things happened in your building?'

Still treading water and anchoring his weight with both hands, Phuoc was nodding. 'My family lived there while it was being renovated, and I remember many workers dying. So, the owner decided to reassure the tenants by fixing things.'

'Do you mean … fix the building?'

'Not the building. He fixed things by calling in a shaman.'

Sensitive subject matter or not, there was no stopping his curiosity now.

'A shaman? Someone to bless the place?'

'Sort of. Our building had spiritual … what my mother called *deficiencies*. The shaman, he acquired four virgins from the local hospital. Four *deceased* virgins.'

Jaison, who had also been kicking his feet, stopped.

Phuoc said, 'The virgins were buried at the four

corners of our building. To protect the area from bad guests.'

'You mean bad ghosts?'

'Yes. In Feng Shui geomancy, such practices are sometimes used.'

'That's awful. Did it work?'

'It did not. When summer arrived, the bodies of the women became exposed by heat. The shaman, he was arrested. Later, my parents became victims of bad luck themselves and disappeared. With nowhere to live and my grandmother in ill health, I was given to a state orphanage.'

They were a short distance from each other (the width of a pool), but Jaison could see Phuoc's expression clearly enough: suffering and resignation combined. Whatever calamities the boy had endured, he appeared reconciled to his fate in life.

'It was a long time ago,' Phuoc said. 'Truth be told, I was very young and don't remember much. Besides, what goes on here is sometimes worse.'

Here it comes.

'What do you mean by that, Phuoc? Is there bad luck inside the castle?'

From across the water, Phuoc's brown eyes looked aghast.

'Are you telling me you *haven't* seen stuff? Like frightening stuff? Selena calls it the elephant in the room. Or elephant in the castle, I suppose you'd say. Apparently, everybody who lives here knows something isn't right. But nobody wants to talk about it.'

Spoken insouciantly, the revelation was like an alarm blaring.

'Do *you* want to talk about it?' Jaison asked.

Phuoc considered this … then gravitated toward the shallow end of the pool. Again on solid footing, he turned back and looked at Jaison solemnly.

'I'm not really sure. I might get into trouble if I do.'

'With whom?'

'With my brother, for starters. All of this … it really began when he arrived.'

No prizes for guessing which brother.

Deciding to tread lightly, Jaison asked, 'He came after you and Selena, didn't he? He was the last one to be fostered?'

'I arrived shortly after Selena. But Montha came from Haiti a year later. From what I understand, there were a lot of problems with my parents' application. At the eleventh hour, there was a big fire in the orphanage he was living in. Many children and matrons died. Montha survived.'

'May I ask how you know all this?'

Again, that forlorn shrug … and Jaison felt a pang of regret at his earlier observation – that Phuoc was some kind of riddle. More or less, the boy was a bystander whose polite civility evinced innocence.

'Word travels in the castle. You hear things.'

'And see things …' Jaison muttered.

'So, you *have* seen something?'

Strangely, his first instinct was to deny the truth. Of course, it was the adult within – wired to seek rational answers. Especially when dealing with a kid.

Ghosts didn't exist.

The boogeyman wasn't real.

No more untruths, Jaison thought.

'There was something in the library. Something alive.'

'Did you recognize it?'

'What do you mean?'

'Some of the stuff I've seen … it's like it's taken from my head. There was one day – I was on the third floor near the lift. Not doing anything much. The lift doors, I saw they were open. I got closer. And there was somebody *inside* the lift.'

'Who?'

'A soldier. He was mostly in uniform. *Mostly*. Not his arms – they weren't covered up. His arms didn't have any skin on them.'

Jesus.

Schooled in Western culture, Jaison surmised the boy had seen an American soldier – some old-school Marine.

But Phuoc's next words demonstrated his naivety.

'I could see he was Viet Cong … and it was like the soldier had appeared from one of my grandma's stories. My Bà ngoại, she told many tales that frightened me. In one of them, ARVN patrols close to her home executed one of their enemies by burning him alive. And afterward, using bayonets, they peeled off his skin like it was a pig.'

Vivid hallucinations could be brought on by nightmares.

This was something Jaison knew intimately from his drinking days.

Enduring withdrawal, his personal symptoms were often a cavalcade of dark phantasms, each more disturbing than the last.

Such illusions were not uncommon for a human body purging a toxic brew.

Jaison refused to insult Phuoc's intelligence by suggesting his encounter with the soldier had been a hallucination.

Jaison asked, 'And then what happened?'

As though a weight had lifted, the boy looked relieved.

'He stepped out. At first, I was curious, thinking his arms were a trick of the light. But as he came forward, he turned around fully and showed me the other side of his body.

'His head … it was charred but still wet. And I could see his brain through missing parts of the skull. I could see it *throbbing*.'

Despite his present environment, Jaison felt tethered to Phuoc's hallway– could easily conjure a dead soldier bereft of skin.

'Seeing that, I wasn't curious anymore. I turned around and ran to the stairs as fast as I could. Going down them, I tripped. When I looked up, he was also on the stairs, following me. His burnt skin … it was sliding off like animal fat. I stood up and started running again. This time, I didn't look back until I got to the first floor.'

Attempting to stand, Jaison discovered his submerged feet were not up to task. 'Have you told anybody else about this?'

Phuoc gave him a measured look. 'I don't think I have. At least, I haven't told anybody about the soldier. But there have been other things – too many to count.'

The boy took a moment to exit the water, and Jaison used the pause to consider what he would say next.

After Phuoc returned with a towel, he asked, 'You said before you felt the soldier was taken from your head. Are you saying the *house* read your mind? That it somehow knows what scares you?'

'Whether it was the house itself or some other thing, I still haven't decided. Maybe if you tell me what you saw in the library, we will both be closer to having an answer.'

Jaison took a moment to think. 'It was between

bookshelves. Some sort of creature. But I had a feeling it wasn't a *regular* animal. I got a little closer to the thing … and saw something with golden eyes.'

'Did you get the feeling this creature was … familiar? Like something from your past?'

The question prompted Jaison to recall his notes.

And one revelatory sentence in particular.

What of the strange golden-eyed apparition which – it pains me to admit – somehow felt familiar?

'Yes. I concede that it felt … personal.'

During their exchange, Phuoc dried himself. On the tiles, his life jacket lay discarded. 'Last week, after we spoke, I also visited the library. And I took a copy of your novel.'

'You mean *Parasites*?'

'I read the whole thing over a couple of nights. I thought it was pretty scary; it makes me wonder …'

'What?'

'If perhaps what you saw in the library that day were your own creations.'

Those golden eyes half-glimpsed …

Jaison's horror novel *Parasites* concerned mutated, gremlin-like creatures that came into existence after being exposed to a certain chemical substance. Before their malign transformation, they were an undiscovered species as docile as domesticated dogs.

These imaginary monsters – despite having evolved from his subconscious – always disturbed him.

During the writing process, he often dreamt of their golden eyes and spittle-slicked jaws.

Inside the library and returned to the first floor, Jaison recalled a reverberation coming from above.

Perhaps the sound he heard had been the mystery creature transforming into the namesake of his novel.

Changing into a *Parasite*.

Phuoc's theory, already feeding a fevered imagination, did not explain his encounter with the mirror man.

Or the existence of a phantom midget boy.

Without realizing it, Jaison noticed Phuoc had crept closer. 'Can I ask you something else?'

Jaison blinked. 'Sure.'

'We've been discussing our mutual fears, things that frighten us. The monsters of your book were frightening, yes. But I want to know what *truly* scares you.'

Jaison stared into the water, considering. The pool filter, a soporific hum, made him feel languid and half-asleep. Then, knowing his reply would raise more questions, simply said, 'Corpse water.'

'Did you say *corpse* water?'

'I did. When I was young – around ten, I think – I fell into a pool of water where something had died. Several somethings, actually.'

Phuoc said nothing.

'You mentioned there were natural swimming holes near your village. In Western Australia, where I grew up, we had them too. What used to be an old mining quarry. After the quarry was abandoned, parts of it would fill up with rainwater. When summer arrived, there was still plenty of water that hadn't evaporated. Local kids used old machinery as a diving board to jump in and cool off. One day, I went for a dip like always … and discovered I'd landed in something that was only *partially* water.'

'Your … corpse water?'

Jaison nodded. 'A mass of decomposing tissue – the rotting remains of what I later discovered was all manner of roadkill. When I first jumped in, I opened my eyes underwater for the briefest moment.'

Phuoc appeared fascinated. 'What did you see?'

'I saw ribcages and bloody torsos. There were even floating eyeballs staring back at me.'

The boy produced a low whistle.

'At first, I didn't think they were dead animals. Dead *humans*, instead. When I came up for air, I was screaming, because who *wouldn't* be? I'd just taken a swan dive into a pool of roadkill.'

Telling his tale, Jaison realized this was no ordinary confession – far from it. Essentially, he was releasing a certain memory that had (up until now) remained dormant. And choosing to disclose this trauma to a stranger (a child, no less), left him feeling spent.

Was it Phuoc's confession that had prompted his own?

Or was it the castle itself, working a weird magic?

Despite the story having an undeniable catharsis, Jaison could almost taste that befouled water from his childhood.

Could envision a reflective surface slick with gore.

Afterward, his mother had taken him to the emergency room where an unsympathetic doctor declared the only lingering symptom from falling in would be psychological.

Lifting his legs from the water at last (and grimacing at his shriveled toes), Jaison stood upright. He said, 'I think it's time to go back to my rooms, Phuoc. Maybe tomorrow you can tell me how –'

He froze.

And gaped at the place where Phuoc had been standing moments ago.

A frantic study of the pool revealed no flailing Phuoc having recently fallen in. A quick glance at the immediate surrounds exposed no boy draped in a towel.

No puddle of water served as evidence he'd been present at all.

Impossible.

On the brink of panicking, Jaison couldn't help but recall more of his notes.

Scribbled prose floating the possibility that Oaklyn Castle was devoid of all life but his own.

Phuoc had *never* been in the pool.

This entire time Jaison had been conversing with air.

Not convinced, it suddenly made sense to escape this room as swiftly as possible.

Retrieving his shoes, Jaison crept toward the exit.

Earlier, the statues appeared malign.

Now Jaison could imagine them cognizant, their demanding visages displeased.

A short distance from freedom, he heard splashing sounds coming from the shallow end of the pool.

It's the kid. He jumped back in when I wasn't looking.

But spinning around, Jaison observed nothing.

Only clear water turned a charcoal green: a churning mass of gelatinous forms like limbs drenched in oil.

Corpse water.

Surely more illusion.

Trickery every bit as tangible as parasite monsters sprung to life.

Against his will, Jaison felt himself being carried back toward the pool.

Where the water had turned crimson.

Filled with a stew of flesh far removed from roadkill.

Dismembered legs and arms.

Rotting skulls and torsos.

Close to crying out, Jaison felt hands on his back.

Pushing him forward to fall.

10

Great events define great spaces.

These were Arabella's words, mentioned as she and Declan scrutinized the grand ballroom of Oaklyn Castle during his first week inside the mansion.

At that time, the space was almost entirely bare.

The ballroom's only claim to real extravagance? Three Italian chandeliers that hung from its ceiling like giant, inverted wedding cakes.

Despite Arabella's long-ago boast, Declan could not recall a single grand event taking place within this room.

No balls or parties.

A vast area of silk shantung walls and hardwood floors, the ballroom remained (for the most part) free of people and furniture.

At the rear, mullioned doors gave access to three separate balconies.

Layered lighting from the chandeliers illuminated a central bar.

The barren slab, bereft of bottles, emphasized a part of the castle essentially abandoned.

It was one of the reasons Declan spent so much time here.

Somehow, the ballroom acted as a barrier to the castle's supernatural phenomena.

No sobbing children.

No time jumps.

For now, the room was an island of rationality in a sea of chaos.

And resistant to whatever Hoodoo Montha had orchestrated for the residents.

To insulate himself further against any potential weirdness (including being transported to other parts of the house), Declan played soft music on a portable radio and sipped gin.

Glass after glass of Bombay Sapphire.

What his friend Oliver Goldman used to call *Mother's Blue Ruin*.

'On account of the blue bottle,' Declan muttered, sipping his drink with practiced ease. 'And its maternal history, of course. Gin was a drink that was consumed by the poorest mothers in England, striving to fend off the cold and hunger of an ancient world.'

When Declan giggled, the sound of his laugh ricocheted around the ballroom like echoes from a deep well.

The sound was undeniably ominous.

Enough Bombay Sapphire coursed through his blood that Declan could ignore what it represented …

Being alone and juiced up in a giant room.

Three drinks later, he came to the abrupt realization he *wasn't* alone.

A man stood behind the empty bar.

***

All the gin in the world could not force him to disregard this new development.

Or alleviate his fear.

Standing by the balcony doors, Declan was still close enough to ascertain the man's shape was not the writer's in residence.

Not Jaison Winters.

Which left one alternative.

His bald friend with the gold-flecked eyes was back.

So much for the ballroom being a barrier.

His speech slurred, Declan whispered, 'Nosferatu has entered the building.'

If the shape behind the bar heard this, he showed no sign.

His vision, amending to the murk, was able to distinguish the outline of a rounded head lacking hair.

Rigid shoulders suggested somebody outfitted

in a black ensemble.

Cautiously edging closer, luminous eyes were soon revealed.

Sober, there could be little doubt Declan would avoid a confrontation. Presently inebriated, he felt equipped to approach the bastard and do battle.

Restricted from leaving the castle – in essence, a *prisoner* – Declan was a man deserving of answers.

Having crept within earshot of the vampire man, he expected his silhouette to evaporate … or at least dissolve into some form of desired bat.

Instead, he appeared to become *more* solidified, a gleaming pate reflecting the chandeliers above.

Two stools were positioned in front of the dust-covered bar.

With a gloved hand, the vampire specter pointed to one.

He's suggesting I take a seat?

If Declan wasn't scared, the moment might be comical.

Nosferatu wants to talk.

Any doubts he *could* talk were laid to rest when the man said: 'Good evening, caregiver. It's been a while since we've crossed paths, has it not?'

The voice, much like the outfit, was in keeping with a different period. Educated and nuanced, the accent contained enough gravitas to be English.

Holding his glass, Declan walked up to the

proffered stool and sat down.

When the vampire smiled, his amber eyes glowed.

'While you are not obliged to say anything, you are, nevertheless, an easy man to read.'

'How so?'

'That glass of yours is almost empty. And you might be wondering, since I'm standing behind a bar, if I'm capable of serving you more.'

Declan said nothing.

'Alas, I cannot. But I can provide you with insights.'

Suddenly, the urge to flee was overpowering.

But Declan quashed the impulse.

During other encounters, the vampire had been elusive. Essentially, unable to touch. Now, his physical substance was proximate – close enough to study by layered light.

Smiling with the same sardonic mirth he'd shown in the theater, the vampire said, 'You're wondering if I'm going to hurt you?'

'Are you?'

'I'll admit my appearance would suggest so. But for now, have no fears. My purpose and function here … would you believe remains a mystery even to me?'

Faint radiance, almost a silver, speckled the vampire's forehead.

Cheeks the color of chalk appeared jaundiced,

the pigments yellowed.

With no real forethought, Declan asked, 'Are you a ghost?'

Uncovering serrated teeth, the thing smiled.

'You're asking me if I'm dead? Did I live here once upon a time? The answer to that, sadly, is no. In truth, I am envious of the condition of ghosts. For there is freedom in that blessed state, is there not? To be able to flit between the years unencumbered by time?'

Declan laughed. Feeling as though his brain floated somewhere above his head, he said, 'You don't have to be a ghost to accomplish *that* feat. Believe me, I speak from experience. If you're not a traditional phantom or vampire, what does that make you? And why have you signaled me out?'

'As I understand it, there are others in the mansion who are as conscious of me as you are. And not everybody sees the same thing.'

'What does *that* mean?'

'It means the power in this place is particular. You might say it *caters* to each individual. Perhaps Selena sees me as a shaman. Maybe her brother looks upon a dying soldier. Just who is my progenitor and inventor? Deep within, I wonder if there are elements of Arabella inside me. Once, before their metamorphosis, those children under your wing may have had a hand in my design.'

Declan could find little logic in this answer;

however, certain words raised alarm bells.

Those children under your wing.

Repressed until now, he felt anger surfacing.

Rage brought into being by a caregiver's instinct to protect Kingston and Vanita.

'You speak of the power in this place. What power are you talking about?'

'I think you know the answer to that, caregiver. The power in Oaklyn Castle is the very same one that's preventing you from walking out the door.'

What sprung into Declan's mind then, evoked from the vampire's reply, was an image of the house itself.

Oaklyn Castle as a conscious creature.

One grown thick with tentacles and vines.

It breathed, this creature.

And its limbs searched for prey.

But presuming the house to be a pivot of power is a mistake I've made before.

'Are you're talking about the boy outside? You're talking about Arabella's son?'

'Perhaps … perhaps not. But he's not *really* her son, is he? No, Montha was born to unassuming parents a world away from here. Montha … a boy of great power and strength manhandled away from his homeland.'

'His homeland? You mean –'

'Montha's birthplace was a realm where his special gifts might have been nurtured. The country of Haiti, though penurious, would have served as an important incubator.'

'An incubator? What for?'

'To refine a transcendent species of evolution. The hardships there … were supposed to work to his advantage. It was unfortunate, in the end, how things came to pass.'

Even inebriated, Declan managed to decipher some meaning here. In a nutshell, this creature was attempting to paint Montha as some kind of messianic being possessing power.

A transcendent species of evolution.

Was such a thing feasible?

The boy had the demeanor of a disgruntled child.

But …

Declan could admit to the likelihood that Montha was capable of so much more.

It remained possible he was the wizard pulling levers and turning dials behind the haunted curtain of the castle.

'You're speaking of his relocation to America?'

'He never wanted this. Never wanted to see the inside of these walls. Arabella sensed a greatness in him – a power. And like a spoiled whore, she had to have a piece of that power. Endowed with privilege, she never saw a human being standing inside that orphanage. She saw a prize she could spirit away.

Something to hang on her walls ... to own.'

Declan wanted to speak.

But the vampire's words were a catalyst for silence.

Having known the starlet for years, he seldom heard punitive judgment concerning her motivations. Yes, Arabella possessed naysayers in the outside world (tribes of them), yet brazen criticism leveled from *this* entity felt like condemnation from the devil himself.

Since his first brush with Arabella – literally bumping into her – Declan remained resolute in supporting his friend.

A person in her corner, on her team.

Admit it. You've always looked upon some of her actions with a certain disdain.

Sown from the seeds of her long-dead mother, Arabella's desire to adopt felt innocuous.

But simmering beneath the surface of every professional actress was a kind of altruism fashioned by clever manipulation.

A desire to foment a pristine profile in keeping with how a philanthropist superstar *should* be.

'You're attempting to engender doubt in my mind when it comes to my employer and friend, aren't you? But it won't work. Because I see through the lies of this place. I see through the illusion.'

Shifting a step closer, the creature zeroed in.

Though a divide of enameled wood separated them, Declan felt himself flinch.

'Is that *so*?' said the vampire. 'Tell me then, caregiver, how is it that after everything you've seen and experienced, you've never once approached your *friend* with what you know? You're trapped here, unable to escape, and bringing this out into the open is taboo? Why don't you admit it to yourself that you no longer trust her?'

Rebuked, Declan stared at the man.

Endeavoring to shift the subject, he asked, 'And what is that I know, exactly? What could I possibly say? That I get drunk and palaver with a thing that looks like a creature of the night? That I fall asleep to ghostly sobbing and –'

'Confess only what your heart knows to be true.'

'And what's that?'

'That Oaklyn Castle has now become sentient thanks to the mind of a prodigious young man. Sentient and unpredictably dangerous. But even now, this same man labors and builds to undo what he originally created.'

Montha is building something ...

Over the past few months, these words haunted him.

'What is he doing out there?'

'You took steps to perform a rescue, didn't you? You summoned a writer to potentially save you? But Jaison is *not* your salvation, caregiver. Only *Montha* can save you.'

For a moment, there was a spark.

Beginning to remember, he glimpsed another image.

Not of the house.

A giant staircase made of stone.

One leading to nowhere.

It was an elusive picture to hold, like something on the tip of his tongue.

Had he *seen* these stairs?

Or dreamt about them?

'That day outside. Or was it somewhere else? I think I saw some kind of staircase ...'

Impelled by this epiphany, the vampire watched him knowingly. 'But it wasn't just one, was it? You saw *many* staircases, didn't you? Each one random, but seemingly part of an ambitious design.'

The words were a harbinger; Declan glimpsed a vision more elaborate than a simple image.

A *throng* of staircases.

Hundreds hugging the castle like a disassembled mountain.

Elbowed together in such profusion, some stairs reached the heights of a skyscraper. Others were jostled together like a child's building blocks – their frameworks fragile.

Despite the vista feeling familiar, Declan knew

this wasn't the past.

It was a future *coming* to pass.

***

If the intent of meeting with Declan tonight was to share this particular revelation, then the vampire's task was complete.

Behind the bar, it suddenly began to abandon its congenial façade.

Hooked incisors suddenly grew savage.

You're wondering if I'm going to hurt you? the vampire had asked earlier.

Perhaps this whole time it had been in a state of conflict, keeping at bay its predatory urges.

Now it was letting go of the pretense.

And shedding what little humanity it possessed.

Hearing clothing rip, Declan observed grey fingernails grow to the size of talons.

The transformation was swift, but it was enough to get Declan off his stool and moving.

Halfway across the ballroom, his foot collided with an empty bottle of Bombay Sapphire.

Blue glass exploded.

Annulling the sound of hissing and splintering wood.

When Declan reached the hallway and imminent escape, only one thing occupied his mind.

It's time to visit Jaison Winters.

And tell him the truth about everything.

<u>11</u>

Jaison dreamt of stairs.

Outside his bedroom, someone (or something) had buttressed a massive staircase against Oaklyn Castle.

Concrete steps reached all the way to his window.

Their purpose, he realized, to gain access to *his* room.

Desperate and eager to forestall any would-be assailant, Jaison used his bedside lamp to break a window.

Cold air rushed in.

Peering down through jagged glass, he spied the midget scaling the steps.

Jumping from one step to another, it would not be long before the dwarfish creature arrived at Jaison's window to dole out harm.

To his left, something else demanded attention.

The pond.

Filled to overflowing with the skeletal and liquid remains of dead things in a churning soup of viscera.

He recalled a similar sight both in his past and recently at the pool.

Tumbling into the fetid mass against his will.

To see the pond succumb to the same dissolution wasn't surprising, really. Oaklyn Castle, somewhat idle since his arrival, was in the process of ramping up its terrors.

Giving the writer a taste of his fears.

As haunted houses were wont to do.

Through the broken window came the sound of drumming footsteps.

His hands fisted into claws; the midget's approach was imminent.

Reaching the final steps, the thing removed its hood.

To reveal a walrus mustache of dirty whiskers.

Bloodshot eyes rimmed an orifice crowded with funnel-like suckers.

Twisting in his bed, Jaison cried out.

***

For some time, the dream lingered. Before showering, Jaison went through a process of checking his bedroom doors and windows.

Days ago, Ophelia gifted him with a small pair of binoculars – complimentary with a dinner tray – and he retrieved them to scour the pond and its accompanying lawns.

No carcasses were contained in the water.

And no stairs buttressed the building.

But there's Vanita, playing alone.

Donned in a bright yellow dress at odds with the weather, the girl was skipping around the water's edge.

It wasn't the first time he'd seen her alone (occasionally Kingston was also present), yet this morning it seemed …

Neglectful.

One small slip, and Vanita would plunge beneath the water.

An avoidable demise having the trappings of a dozen headlines.

Which led to thoughts of his own descent into a pool.

A fall facilitated by someone's assertive hands.

At least they'd felt like hands.

But Jaison couldn't be certain.

Could not be sure those events by the pool had transpired as he remembered them.

Had Phuoc been present?

Or had the boy been as illusory as a pool of corpse water?

There was no way of knowing the truth.

Because he'd not seen Phuoc since.

In the aftermath of falling in, Jaison had woken up on a second-floor hallway, his skin dry.

He had no memory of walking or being carried there.

According to his phone, hours had passed.

Feeling perturbed, he'd slowly crept back to his rooms.

Sure in the knowledge there was nothing wrong with him.

***

In the cold light of a new morning, this rationale was harder to accept.

Perhaps there *was* something wrong with him.

Perhaps, after decades of hard boozing, Jaison Winters was finally succumbing to the mental deficiencies prevalent among the drunkards of the world.

Brain damage would go a long way to explaining his experiences in Oaklyn Castle … and his inability to adhere to the kind of solid work ethic he'd achieved in the past.

My biography on Arabella.

Staring at his handwritten notes and laptop, it was easy to conclude the whole project was essentially worthless.

While it was true Jaison's time in the castle had been short, it would also be accurate to say he'd absorbed nothing crucial concerning Arabella and her personal proclivities.

Most of his accumulated notes seemed apropos to the house.

So do what Declan advised against doing. Sit down and write a book called The Haunting of Oaklyn Castle.

The old Jaison would have swiftly discarded the idea.

But everything changed that morning upon discovering the secret tunnel.

***

During his wanderings, Jaison discovered most guest rooms (including his own) had Persian floor rugs over tea-stained floors.

On any given day, pacing, he'd noticed one floorboard contained a noticeable creak.

As it grew progressively louder, he decided at last to inspect the offending beam.

Furniture repositioned, Jaison proceeded to roll up the main carpet. On his knees (and through a process of knocking), he discovered additional loosened boards over a broad area.

Further examination revealed he stood on a horizontal doorway.

A secret hatch camouflaged by carpets.

***

In thriller films and novels, secret passageways

were often prevalent, their reasons for existing to conceal sinister machinations.

Inset with a gold handle, this door remained keeping with the ominous intrigues of a film.

Did every guest room in the castle contain one?

Or have I been coaxed to the sole outlet?

After a few moments of indecision, Jaison grabbed the handle and pulled upward.

***

Expecting something portentous (perhaps a blast of ancient wind), Jaison was instead greeted with a nondescript set of stairs, perhaps a dozen in total. Seeing this small variety, after the leviathan of his dreams, was enough to bring a smile.

Meager daylight illumined lime-green tiles.

Before going down, he listened intently for anything that might reveal the nature of the space.

Aside from outside wind at the bedroom window, there was nothing.

You're going down there without a flashlight?

Ophelia, having gifted him with binoculars, failed to provide her new guest with something as rudimentary as matches.

Why would she? You're here to write a novel – not partake of ghost-hunting adventures.

Guardedly, Jaison entered the narrow space.

Which expanded to the dimensions of a

corridor.

One leading west.

Behind the stairs, an arbitrary wall served as a dead end.

His steps tentative, Jaison envisioned the door slamming shut, a dwarfish midget set on barring his return.

This has been under me the whole time – another realm beneath my bed.

Of course, this was true of all places everywhere; the hidden kingdoms you were oblivious to on a day-to-day basis. An unseen labyrinth of pipes, plumbing, and underground sewers seldom glimpsed.

On Jaison's right, the suggestion of a doorway.

A rectangular arch festooned with the light of a dozen burning candles.

By their luminescence, he could see at least three people crowding around an assortment of furniture.

Black outlines embossed on grey, they were like cardboard cutouts.

Two women standing.

A male sitting down.

When the figures made no effort to move, Jaison breathed again.

Because these weren't real people.

Revealed in flickering candlelight, he perceived mannequins poised around a table, their body language reflecting camaraderie.

Strangely, this didn't have the hallmarks of Owen Hedley's experiment, this being a portion of the house that remained undiscovered until now.

No, this felt entirely recent.

In surprise, Jaison moaned.

His initial supposition – the mannequins were a family – seemed correct.

Crude representations of Arabella, Ophelia, and Declan were gathered around a dining table.

Though the dummies were decayed, there was enough familiarity to understand who was being mimicked in the tableau.

The Ophelia mannequin stood in the process of setting down a plate.

Grinning a cracked and painted smile, a Declan mannequin accepted the offering.

Frozen in the act of illustrating a joke, an ersatz Arabella had her arms outstretched.

Each sported a dirty wig.

Except Ophelia.

Though bald, enough tan paint covering the plastic flesh left little doubt who was being mirrored.

Burning candles indicated the presence of someone close.

Despite the peril, Jaison's curiosity was overwhelming.

Who the fuck put this together? What's the

point?

Approaching the table, a dozen theories struggled for traction.

What came to the forefront of everything were Voodoo dolls.

Which led to thoughts of Amelia in her chapel.

And Selena's book.

One concerning Haitian Voodoo.

For a moment, he felt the mystery at the heart of the castle unraveling, a puzzle box on the precipice of being solved.

What essential detail am I missing?

An epiphany too slippery to grasp, the pieces refused to fall into place.

Neglected until now, the remaining parts of the room had his full attention.

Serving as candle holders, there was a mishmash of old and new furniture.

What he felt, what he *perceived*, was something created this scene as a kind of homage; an unsophisticated attempt to pay reverence to the beings who lived above.

Frayed in places, the mannequins' clothes were the real thing.

Garments filched from their real-life counterparts.

Sparkling on fiberglass hands and throats, jewelry was also prevalent.

Beneath the vacant gaze of the Declan doll, a

book lay open like a stage prop.

Intent on getting a closer look, he was stopped short by a twist of movement.

Ophelia, craning her head to follow his movement.

***

Further down the hallway, another room.

Reaching it, Jaison almost convinced himself he'd imagined the first.

Mannequins did not move on their own.

No, they did not.

But the same rationale could be applied to his other encounters.

Mirror men did not appear from the past.

Pools of water did not suddenly fill with cadavers.

As though the memory were a catalyst, rotting scents abruptly filled the air.

Candle smoke … and mold and fungus trappings.

But there was also something else beneath the status quo – a tang like spoiled plant life or rotting eggs.

This room, containing a door, had contents no less disturbing.

Straw-stuffed scarecrows.

The props on display were himself and the

gardener.

Like the previous room, the scarecrows were crudely assembled.

But telltale signs somebody had made *his* likeness were abundantly clear.

It's wearing my clothes.

A black jumper and jeans; the same ensemble Jaison was wearing when he'd visited Amelia's Hoodoo shrine.

Makeshift overalls tangled with straw gave leeway the other effigy was modeled after the gardener.

A single bulb illuminated walls covered in arcane symbols and crosses – the likeness here was juvenile.

A child's attempt to parody the real thing.

Nobody else had been present that afternoon.

But somebody *must* have been.

To concoct this elaborate display, Jaison and Amelia had been observed up close.

Montha?

A likely candidate; somehow, the kid didn't feel right.

Exactly why, Jaison couldn't say … a gut feeling more than anything else told him both rooms were the handiwork of a force with less feeling than a thinking human.

As if the dioramas were churned out at the behest of an algorithm.

But someone stole your wardrobe. Then returned here and dressed up this fucking nightmare. If not Montha, then who?

Filling his sinuses again, the rotting stench had ripened enough to make him gag. With watering eyes, Jaison retreated to the corridor – a passage bright with the fecund glow of an underground cave.

What now?

Withdraw back to his room?

Or discover what other oddities were lying in wait?

What determined his decision was the odor.

Having once fallen into a weir of roadkill, Jaison was intimate with the smell of decomposition.

Further down, something had died.

And he had no choice but to discover what.

***

A house within a house.

Going deeper into the labyrinth, this was Jaison's impression.

Corridors branched off from more corridors, each one containing additional rooms. While most were devoid of anything but floorboards and dust, others featured additional mimicries of life within Oaklyn Castle.

In one room, he stumbled across a Selena mannequin.

Choosing not to linger, he established the doll was engaged in intercourse, partnered with another who looked like Phuoc.

Had such a pairing transpired in real life?

Giving no thought to choosing left over right, his decision based on the whim of nerves, it wasn't long before Jaison came upon the source of the stench.

At the end of another corridor, a bundled thing.

Roughly the size of a large dog and covered with a grey sheet.

Above the wrapped form, an oblong of light filtered down from a tinted window.

Upon closer inspection, Jaison was forced to cover his nose and mouth.

The sheet isn't grey, he thought, inching forward to complete a task his body and mind rebelled against. *It's black with blood.*

Also deceptive from afar, he saw the tinted window was two-way glass.

On the other side of the glass could be seen a hallway, carpeted and pristine.

Not so long ago, he walked that hallway.

And afterward, he watched a ghost from the past contemplate its final moments.

I'm on the other side of the gilded mirror.

Like ripping off a bandage, Jaison reached

down and peeled back the sheet.

Revealing the bodies of children.

A boy and a girl.

Flesh had gone to putrefaction.

Mouths locked in silent screams; the cadavers stared up at Jaison with eyes like solid marble.

Once tender throats had been flayed, the cause of death disclosed.

During his approach down the corridor, Jaison had never (not even for a moment) contemplated the possibility the shrouded dead might belong to Kingston and Vanita.

<u>12</u>

<u>*Notes: The Authorized Biography of Arabella Jaqus.*</u>

I am not a composed man.

In truth, it's staggering how I can sit here writing.

Put simply: I am not tranquil enough to write with surefooted confidence.

What I am is terrified.

Which seems almost absurd to say at this divide, doesn't it?

As if a mirror man isn't frightening enough.

As if being chased by a deformed midget isn't sufficient motivation to leave the castle for good.

And there's the issue of discovering the twins are dead.

Surely this finding will serve as a catalyst to see me out the front door for good ...

***

It turns out, it was enough.

My journey through the house within a house featured different manmade nightmares, stumbling across those cold and lifeless bodies was the final straw.

So, I attempted to leave.

Attempted being the operative word.

Fearful of getting lost, I found my way back to the door contained within my floor easily enough.

Shaky and dry-mouthed, I rolled the Persian over my floorboards as swiftly as I had peeled the rug back.

My bedroom, banal in the details, appeared sinister under the dark light of what I now knew to be true.

Through my eyes, I saw a large bed – acknowledged the writing table covered with notes.

But I also saw, sunk deep into the orbit of small skulls, the dead eyes of Kingston and Vanita.

I struggled to banish the image of their torn throats.

Arabella's children, savagely cut down and hidden away like garbage.

Until now, the castle had granted me many illusions.

So, what made me arrive at the conclusion those bodies were really the twins?

Call it an instinctual knowing.

A certainty I still believe now.

The children are dead.

This whole time, I've have been interacting with ghosts.

Are they aware they're dead?

From everything I've observed, I feel Kingston and Vanita are spirits ignorant of their condition.

By default, does this make the other residents – Arabella, Ophelia, Declan and Amelia – also ghosts?

Are Selena and Phuoc apparitions?

My intuition tells me no.

Leaving my room, I gave no forethought to taking personal possessions with me. There are my notes, of course – but in my haste to depart I entered the hallway with only the clothes on my back.

Always in the rear of my mind, I anticipated being stopped before reaching the front door.

Perhaps a decaying version of Arabella would attempt to block my escape, her marble eyes sunken like her offsprings' ...

But I encountered no such obstacles.

For the first time since stepping into the mansion, I stood among the sculpted bushes I'd observed from a limousine window a thousand years ago.

Hadn't the nameless driver remarked they appeared phallic?

Yes, I believe he had ... yet navigating a route that would see me escape, I felt those memories were inconsequential and belonged to another man.

A short time later, I approached the black gates of Oaklyn Castle. These gates, concealed unless you are in close proximity, are like something from Arabella's menagerie of movies: a medieval monstrosity of steel points and winged crucibles.

Stretching away on the other side: a nondescript dirt road.

A real and tangible world away from this accursed family.

Walking up to prod a baluster, I knew it was a world I wouldn't be permitted to return to.

More intuition?

Touching the gate would confirm my worst fears.

Because suddenly I was returned to the castle.

***

If this were a novel of fiction, perhaps I would recount a great physical sensation to accompany my transition, a gravity tide enveloping both body and consciousness. In the aftermath of the supernatural fire, I might awaken with limbs like jelly and a feeling of being passed through some ghostly birth canal.

No such impressions attended my displacement.

One moment, I was on the precipice of freedom.

The next, I awoke in the house as if awakening from a dream.

To find myself on a carpeted floor beside a gilded mirror.

Whatever force had orchestrated this jaunt, it had seen fit to place me in the proximity of dead children.

Separated solely by inches of two-way glass.

Knowing what lay on the other side, I did not linger long.

Prudence would dictate I return to my rooms – in my frustration and terror, I yearned to find another face.

Anyone or anything that could guarantee my existence by sharing a brief piece of their own.

But no one could be found.

Not Selena in the library.

Not Ophelia in her kitchens.

The hallways were as silent as catacombs.

As if, after all, I had always been the sole occupant.

Hesitant of my rooms – and what lay beneath them – I eventually returned to begin these notes.

While I remain ignorant of my circumstances, it appears there are rules I must live by.

I can venture outside.

But am forbidden to leave the castle proper.

One thing I remain convinced of: some of the residents are no longer alive.

There is so much to contemplate.
Is Montha the engine that powers everything?
What is the significance of his random stairs?
Will any human eyes read these words if I
remain trapped here?
Presently, I hear sounds coming from outside.
A woman screaming.
It seems I'm not alone after all.

<u>13</u>

Nails were driven into the soft portion of the gardener's palms.

Buttressed against the eastern wall of the chapel, Amelia's overall-clad body assumed the carriage of crucifixion. A coagulating pool of blood beneath her feet, in addition to a lolling tongue, gave leeway the gardener was dead.

On Jaison's right stood Arabella.

On his left, Ophelia gaped at Amelia's body with disbelief, her artificial eyelashes fluttering.

Barely audible, he heard Arabella whisper two words.

A name.

Eden Federer.

Amelia's old lover?

The handyman. She's naming the culprit.

***

Earlier, Jaison left the house in a stew of fear.

195

Far away, there were raised voices, a distant scream.

Familiar with the geography from his previous journey, Jaison took the same route to the rear of the castle.

A hodgepodge of dreamlike images fought for dominance in his mind.

Amelia's home, hung with crucifixes.

A burned man inside an elevator.

Severed limbs floating in a recreational pool.

Against apocalyptic skies, Montha standing on stairs.

Dead twins, their throats cut.

Several times, consumed by the sequence of scenes, Jaison lost his footing.

With darkness approaching, creeping twilight transformed this part of the property into a shadow-plagued jungle.

Grey obelisks in the gloom, soon the water fountains came within sight.

For an uncertain moment he thought they were staircases, the unseen armada Montha had mentioned.

Past the pissing cherubs he jogged, knowing his ultimate destination. He'd visited the chapel once before, of course – and even bore witness to a crude reenactment of his time there.

When the building bled into view, Jaison thought he might be viewing more of the same.

Stuffed scarecrow figures.

Then the scarecrows resolved into breathing outlines.

Arabella and Ophelia.

Their attention reserved for the woman nailed to the wall.

***

No tears blemished Arabella's perfect face.

'Amelia was unreachable by phone for hours,' she said. 'Which never happens. So, I came back here to see if she was okay …'

For the first time, Jaison looked over at Ophelia, studied a face also bereft of tears. Had it been Ophelia's scream he'd heard?

This strange reunion engendered a profound sense of unease.

After everything Jaison had recently discovered – and now this fresh development – it was safe to assume he could no longer trust this family.

Flies, having found their prize, began to crawl over Amelia's open wounds.

Pinioned three feet from the ground, someone of great strength must have simply lifted the woman up and stabbed her with nails.

Amelia resembled her bloodied figurines.

Studying the body, Jaison said, 'Did you know she practiced a dark form of spiritualism? Do you think this has something –'

'Hoodoo isn't dark,' said Ophelia. 'And no, her beliefs have nothing to do with this.'

'How do you know? Are the authorities coming? Have you called anyone?'

Silence followed the question.

As though calling the police had not registered for either woman.

Arabella said, 'I have connections with someone local – a detective. But you must understand, Jaison. This is no ordinary house. And we are no ordinary family.'

'I don't understand. You're going to leave her up there? Arabella – if you think your old employee did this, then he's probably still lurking around.'

'Eden Federer was a jealous man,' said Ophelia. 'They had bitter arguments day and night. In the end, this was the reason he was let go. And we always wondered … if he might return.'

'I thought he still worked here?'

'I don't know who told you that,' said Arabella. 'But Boyd escorted him off the property last year.'

He was about to say *Selena*.

But the moment was lost in a tumult of sound.

From the direction of the roof came a vibrating alarum like the weight of something shifting.

Visible to the naked eye, Oaklyn Castle appeared as a watery mirage, the roof a black line of dwarf walls and snow brackets.

The shifting sound repeated.

'I can't begin to imagine what that *was*,' said Jaison. 'Surely you also heard it?'

Again, he was answered with silence.

'Has anyone been inside the chapel yet?'

'Of course,' said Ophelia. 'I made sure it was safe first thing.'

'I think I should take a look around.'

Knowing Arabella might protest, Jaison maneuvered away to the chapel's entrance. Much like the previous visit, he pushed open the unlocked door before anything could interrupt the effort.

*****

The air inside smelt of stale incense, wood smoke, and blood.

Overturned furniture and smashed appliances suggested a savage skirmish.

Amelia put up a fight.

Stepping in, Jaison attempted to paint a picture within his mind.

The gardener struggling against an assailant equipped with hammer and nails. Ripped from the walls, Hoodoo talismans had been thrown to the carpet.

Mesmerized by the blood, Jaison failed at first to recognize the altered wall art.

In place of Adam and Eve, a fresh mural of a

young boy.

A midget.

Through solvents and pigments, Jaison's hooded tormentor brooded.

As in life, his face was shadowed … two embers beneath the cowl could be construed as eyes.

Bright blood spattered his pea-green slicker.

Behind the boy, random stairs stretched to the sky like an abandoned amusement ride.

Engrossed in the painting, Jaison did not hear Ophelia come up behind him. When she placed a hand on his shoulder, he cried out as if stung.

'You shouldn't be in here. You need to leave.'

Jaison pointed a shaking finger at the mural. 'Who did this?'

'It must have been Eden. He was always painting when he wasn't fixing things.'

'He returned here after murdering his old lover and decided to paint the walls?'

More silence.

'Do you know who that boy is?'

'I recognize him, yes.'

'Who is it?'

'Amelia's nephew, Mark.'

Even with everything Jaison had endured so far, this revelation felt like a gut punch.

'Nephew?'

'For a time, Eden and the boy were close. But

something changed. Amelia told us he became cruel to Mark, emotionally as well as physically. It was a final straw that broke their relationship.'

Questions begged to be asked, and Jaison was of a mind to interrogate Ophelia there and then.

Simply push her onto the soiled carpet and demand answers.

Did the boy go missing in the house, Ophelia? Did Eden murder him, too? Because I've been seeing his ghost for weeks now. And he's not happy with me.

But he did none of those things.

Instead, he shifted his eyes to the fireplace where Amelia's trinkets burned.

'She was trying to protect herself from something … and it all came to nothing. What will you do?'

'The question is,' said Ophelia. 'What will *you* do? I trust you will practice the upmost discretion? That you won't make any phone calls of your own before Arabella's had a chance to deal with things?'

What came to mind then were the gardener's frozen eyes – and the pain she must have endured. So far, he'd made no mention of the labyrinth beneath his room. If he was fighting *that* battle alone, then he could adhere to Ophelia's wishes.

'You can trust me,' he said.

'Good. For now, return to the house. Later, either Arabella or I will come and see you when the time is appropriate.'

***

Tempted to take one final look at Amelia, Jaison resisted the impulse.

Arabella had disappeared.

Slowly, he walked back to the mansion.

Sometime later – and close enough to see turrets and windows in detail – Jaison spied the human figure of Declan Avery staring down at him through opaque glass.

<u>14</u>

Evocative of an underground dungeon, the wine cellars of Oaklyn Castle were a world unto themselves. Again, playing tour guide, Declan led Jaison through a labyrinth of tiled floors and plaster ceilings.

A tamper-proof, biometric entry system programmed to accept Declan's fingerprint had granted them access. Walking, he explained the cellars held up to four thousand bottles and were temperature controlled.

'The most impressive detail is the barrel-vaulted ceilings. They use a centuries-old technique to ensure even weight distribution.'

Craning his neck upward, Jaison said, 'On any other day, this might interest me. But I have to ask what we're doing down here?'

The caregiver turned around and regarded Jaison with a sheepish smile. 'I suppose I'm describing all this … to try and stall the inevitable.'

'Which is?'

'A conversation long overdue.'

In every direction, the bottles of booze were like hundreds of leering faces demanding attention.

Which left little doubt Declan was ignorant of his past.

'I agree with you. But why does it have to take place in the wine cellars?'

'My first choice would have been the ballroom. That used to be my ivory tower – a place where I felt safe.'

'Not anymore?'

'No, not anymore.'

Keen for details, Jaison did not press the issue. Possibly, Declan would reveal specifics concerning the ballroom in due time.

'What makes you think the wine cellars are any safer?'

'I don't. But I've never experienced anything remotely supernatural down here. And that has to count for something.'

***

'What if I was to tell you Amelia is dead? Would that shock you?'

They were in a subterranean place of arching stone walls bereft of bottles. A succession of pillars and pointed vaults conveyed the environment was more in keeping with a traditional basement found in an ancient castle.

Remarkably, no surprise registered on Declan's face. He said, 'This is something you witnessed inside the chapel? You saw Amelia's body?'

'I saw her crucified to the wall of her home. Arabella opinioned her ex-lover is responsible. Ophelia agrees with the sentiment. Why isn't any of this shocking you?'

'Let's just say … I've been waiting for something like this to happen. For one of us to be laid low. Because things reached a crisis point some time ago.'

Jaison considered this. 'Things?'

'Last evening, I had a cordial conversation with something in the ballroom. Something that wasn't human. An apparition who's lived here for a while. For months, I've been travelling backward and forward through time. Essentially, I've been shifting to different periods in the mansion's history.'

With these revelations, there was little doubt Declan expected a stunned response.

And Jaison failed to provide it.

'Judging from the look on *your* face, I can only guess you've been fighting a battle of your own.'

'A battle? That doesn't seem like the appropriate word. Where to begin with all I've endured?'

'Begin at the beginning.'

And so Jaison did.

***

First, he recounted his experience in the library, describing everything from the phantom animal to the mirror man.

Then it was on to Amelia's chapel … and how it had come to be a repository for bloodstained trinkets.

He described Montha, the random stairs, and the strange conversation which followed.

Lastly, when the time came to reveal the reality of the midget, Jaison discovered he was barely up to task.

And you're forgetting the worst parts. There's your corpse water. And acknowledging what lies beneath the floorboards …

Through the spiel, Declan remained stoic and nodded in certain places. When Jaison finished talking, the man fixed him with a hard stare.

'You're not telling me everything.'

'I'm not, no.'

'Why not?'

'I don't think I'm ready to. I don't think *you're* ready.'

'You don't think I can handle it?'

'It has the potential to change everything.'

'From what you've told me, everything *has* already changed. Amelia is dead. You said Arabella was calling someone. I don't think that's going to happen, do you?'

He pondered Arabella's response – her words concerning both house and family. Both beyond the natural laws of the world at large.

'You're right … I don't think she'll be making that call. Declan, do you think anyone living here is capable of murder? After my conversation with Montha, I concluded he's a feared presence.'

'Because he *is* a feared presence,' Declan replied, and proceeded to explain his own misgivings, the boy's enigmatic behavior over time.

'But he's human, isn't he? As human as you or me?'

'Do you know what? In a house where I've been trapped and held prisoner for so long, I'm not sure it even matters.'

With the words acting as a trigger, Jaison could feel his environment spinning. Above, ceiling tiles had the hallucinatory traits of a moving chessboard.

Concerned, Declan put out an arm to steady him.

'I'm fine. But I think it's time to tell you everything.'

Most of it came out then, a deluge of words like heaving dark poison.

Attempting to leave via the front gates, then losing consciousness.

Awakening by a hallway mirror where a ghost had stood.

And where children were murdered on the

other side ...

Having no desire to recount his time within the walls, this too came out, a linear description of crypt rooms that contained burning candles and scarecrow mannequins.

'They were us, Declan,' Jaison said, surprised to hear unhinged emotion in his voice. 'They were *us*. Replicas of people under this roof ... including you and me.'

Finally, Declan's expression registered the shock he sought.

Whatever he was expecting me to say, it wasn't this. Physical objects under the thrall of some godlike force.

'But here comes the fun part. There's something else down there ... on the other side of the mirror. Two children.'

'Children?'

'Deceased.'

Something like relief came over the caregiver. 'You unearthed skeletons? This house is *old*, Jaison. Bones have been found before. I'm not surprised you –'

'No, you don't understand. They were not skeletons. Visibly decomposed, yes. I'm not sure how long for. Months. Perhaps more. But not decayed enough to see who they were and how they died.'

In the dungeon gloom, Declan's eyes glistened.

In a soft whisper, he asked, 'Who were they?'

'Kingston and Vanita. Declan, the twins are lying dead within the walls.'

***

'That can't possibly be true,' said Declan.

But Jaison detected doubt in the caregiver's eyes – the revelation was something he'd previously considered.

'The house … I'll grant can summon illusions. Only recently, before I discovered what lay beneath my floorboards, I was shown something from my own past. Basically, the house had me believing Oaklyn's pool was filled with rotting bodies, dozens of them, cut up like cattle. I believe if I returned there now, I would find nothing. But this wasn't *like* that. Declan, I urge you to see what I saw with your own eyes. If you did –'

'No,' said Declan, his voice emphatic. 'You're telling me Kingston and Vanita – the same children who have rooms close to mine – are dead? Then who have I been looking after? Who have I been putting to bed each night? Are you telling me *they're* ghosts?'

Pinned beneath the man's scowl, Jaison looked away.

He felt embarrassed.

Because his words sounded farcical.

Even to my own ears.

'I won't mention that word. But you said before you're a prisoner here. A hostage. Which means you've attempted to leave. Did you black out at the gates? I suppose what I'm trying to say is when compared to that kind of phenomena, how is discovering there may be ghosts any less believable?'

'It wasn't the gates,' Declan said. By now, the caregiver was pacing, massaging a sweaty brow between thumb and forefinger.

'What do you mean?'

'I mean I didn't lose consciousness attempting to open the gates. Jaison, I can't *get* that far. I can't even leave the house. I haven't been able to step out the front door. So yes, I'm a prisoner. And if we're spilling our guts about everything here, that's why I brought you into the equation.'

'I don't get it. Brought me into the equation?'

'I invited you, Jaison. It was my idea. I invited you to Oaklyn Castle for many reasons … but mainly to help me escape.'

Sweet Jesus. He's telling the truth.

Suddenly, Jaison felt himself vulnerable under the weight of Declan's words – exposed in some fundamental way.

Everything he believed until now – his reasons for being summoned (even his ill-defined belief system) seemed like a complete fallacy.

Delusions brought into being by a sober mind hungering for a happy ending after a lifetime of booze.

'I was a desperate man at the end of his tether,' Declan was saying. 'Everything I'd done in an effort to escape my prison – jumping from a window once, if you can believe it – had come to naught.'

'Why didn't you tell someone? From my own experience, I know phones are useless … but why didn't you ask someone here for help?'

Declan cackled, the sound half crazed. 'For the same reason *you* won't ask any of the others for help. Do you trust the Lady of the Manor, Jaison? Do you trust her *children*? Doesn't your gut sometimes tell you they're a part of it all?'

'What about Ophelia? Both of you are *very* close. Surely, she –'

'I thought I was in love with Ophelia. Perhaps I even was, once. But those days are long gone and hard to find.'

Feeling faint again, Jaison swayed on his knees. In a similar manner as Declan, he began to rub his forehead.

'So, what was your plan? You thought by bringing me here I'd somehow know how to rescue you? What did you do? Implant the idea in Arabella's head?'

Declan nodded. 'That's *exactly* what I did. I

know you're not aware of this, but you and I have a lot in common. In a strange way, our lives sort of echo each other. Although you succeeded where I could not.'

'What are you talking about?'

'Before coming to Oaklyn Castle, before my role as caregiver, I lived among the Hollywood elite selling scripts. This is how I met Arabella. And before *that*, I was among the countless millions with dreams of being a novelist. Years ago, I stumbled across your body of work.'

'*You* gave Arabella my books to read?'

Declan ignored the question. 'When she raised the idea of hiring a biographer – essentially have this person live with us like a fly on the wall – it dawned on me you would be the perfect fit. In a nutshell, I decided to appoint you her scribe.

'Of course, I knew the biography in all probability would never be written, much less published. But that didn't matter. What I wanted above everything else was for another human being to experience everything I had; see and feel everything I did.'

'What in God's name *for*? So, you wouldn't feel alone?'

'I suppose so. And to establish I wasn't insane. In this endeavor, if nothing else, I believe I succeeded.'

There were too many admissions at once;

Jaison's head swam even more. While this disclosure was indeed revelatory – and marked a quantum jump in things – it was also true that none of Declan's admissions could help them now.

What Jaison needed were details.

Something to use as ammunition in their effort to escape.

'You said before you spoke to something in the ballroom that wasn't human. What was it?'

Declan grinned … a smile that was both wistful and somehow malign.

'A vampire.'

'A vampire?'

'A creature that bears some resemblance to Nosferatu. A thing that's been stalking me for a while. The first time I saw him was in the theatre, and last night was the first night he spoke to me. Looking back, he didn't offer much insight. Except we seemed to agree about one thing.'

'And what would that be?'

'That somebody under this roof had a hand in his design.'

***

After a drawn-out silence, Jaison and Declan agreed being underground this late was asking for trouble. With Declan again leading, they made their way back to the hallways via a maze of aging wine.

Jaison said, 'Knowing what we know now – and I'll admit we know very little – what would you suggest we do?'

'I've just confessed I'm the reason you're here. Aren't you livid about this?'

Jaison took a moment consider the question, essentially inspect his own feelings. 'Not exactly. I sort of understand your original motivation. Besides, I'm too tired to be angry.'

'You just want to leave?'

'Preferably in one piece.'

Removed from the cellars and returned to the house proper, Jaison could immediately feel the juxtaposition – a sudden pain in his chest and ear canal like mild indigestion.

If he'd previously harbored doubts the house meant him harm, these were eclipsed in the discomfort of the moment.

'I have an idea,' Declan said. 'It's what I was going to do tomorrow night, with or without you.'

'And what would that be?'

'I'm going to confront the monster.'

'You're talking about Oaklyn Castle?'

'I'm talking about Montha.'

Jaison recalled his one interaction with the boy … and managed to suppress a shudder. 'How do you suppose we do that? I'm sure you're aware the boy practically lives outside.'

Declan shook his head. 'His room is on the

fourth floor, the very *last* room on that floor. I think whatever takes up his attention during the day – it's only a part of it. The entire fourth floor is his domain, his territory. It's like the Eagle's Nest of Oaklyn Castle.'

Despite their circumstances, Jaison permitted himself to laugh.

Likening the boy's private realm to Hitler's headquarters didn't feel like such a far-fetched analogy.

'So, we go up to the boogeyman's lair and simply knock on his door? I don't suppose you own a firearm?'

'Arabella doesn't –'

'Believe in guns. Yes, I remember reading about *that*. I guess it doesn't matter, anyway. Because I don't think a weapon will do us any good.'

'Not in these circumstances, no.'

'So, we confront the monster. Does this plan entail anything beyond a heroic idea and wishful thinking for a good outcome?'

'Not exactly. But I no longer believe we have a choice where survival is concerned. The boy … he sleeps at night like anyone else. Tonight, rest. Tomorrow evening, I'll fetch you from your room. Together, we'll take the stairs to the fourth floor.'

Jaison seized on an issue he'd been avoiding until now.

'What about the twins? Will you carry on like normal?'

'Thankfully they're with their mother tonight.'

He sighed. 'There's no way to be prepared for something like this, is there?'

Frowning, Declan measured the question.

And Jaison noted a weariness in the man's expression which belied he was resigned to an uncertain fate.

15

Notes: The Authorized Biography of Arabella Jaqus.

Less than twenty-four hours ago, Ophelia mentioned someone would visit me, a follow-up to the hideous discovery of the crucified gardener.

No one has come.

Where is Arabella now?

Doing damage control? Taking steps to sweep under the rug something that could ruin her family's legacy?

It saddens me I won't get to complete this work in progress, but I have decided to hold onto the words. On this table lies a leather satchel for the handwritten pages, and I will carry these with me into whatever maelstrom awaits us tonight.

Vanita's gift I've decided to leave here.

***

This will be my last entry.

Though I hope to continue adding words, something tells me – call it instinct again – today is my last night inside Oaklyn Castle.

Hours from now, Declan Avery will knock on my door – and we will go as one to confront (or perhaps provoke) the force at the heart of the house's phenomena.

Of course, I could have refused Declan's offer to confront the monster – could have simply resigned myself to more days and nights knowing the twins were murdered, and I cannot leave by traditional means.

With little doubt, the drunkard Jaison Winters of old would have embraced such cowardice.

But I am no longer that man.

Those twelve steps I navigated years ago – cultish rubbish in hindsight – at least taught me the value of confrontation and resolution.

And that is why I will accompany Declan to the fourth floor.

Tonight, there will be new steps to traverse.

A dizzying array of random stairs.

<u>16</u>

When Declan arrived at Jaison's room, there was no need to knock. Like an eager student, the writer stood by his door, a leather satchel roped across his body.

Although he already had an idea, Declan asked, 'What's inside?'

'Most of what I've written. A lot of it just notes, streams of consciousness stuff. I'm not sure why I'm bringing it with me. It would be a shame to lose it all, I suppose.'

'Or let it fall into the wrong hands.'

'That, too.'

'You know we don't have to do this, right? If you think going up to Montha's room is some kind of suicide mission –'

'It's like you said before … if we want to get out of here, there isn't much choice. And I'll feel better if this work-in-progress comes along with me.'

'Fair enough. Shall we do this?'

'Lead the way.'

219

***

Though short, their journey to the apex of the mansion made room for all manner of strangeness.

Gliding the main hallway of the second floor, Declan spied a human figure cowering behind the helmed visor of a plaster knight.

The ghost of the gardener.

A lifeform new to the world at large and confused by its condition.

'I suppose the rules in this haunted mansion are like any other,' Jaison said. 'You die underneath the roof; you wander here forever.'

'Look at her *hands*,' said Declan.

Sheathing the woman's palms, there was an ethereal penumbra of reddish material.

Where the nails pierced, Declan thought sickly.

As he watched, the supernatural mist blossomed into moving spheres like blood viewed in a weightless environment.

'Let's keep moving,' Jaison said.

Arriving on the third floor, they were greeted by the sound of laughter.

Two women, their merriment intertwined.

Halfway down the hallway, the women became visible.

Embracing each other drunkenly, their delight at being observed was obvious.

'This is *long* overdue,' said the girl on the left. Attractive and blond, Declan observed a hint of breast showing through white fabric.

'When you boys eventually join us,' said her dark-haired companion. 'Be sure to come to our rooms for a visit.'

Sniggering, she proceeded to lavish kisses on exposed flesh.

In between her affections, she said, 'Jennifer can abide a man in bed … maybe I can be persuaded, too. Make sure *both* of you come and visit.'

Growing in volume, there was more laughter as both men sauntered past.

'The suicide brides,' Jaison whispered. 'Jennifer and Amy?'

'Don't look back,' said Declan.

He discovered, walking past the couple, that he could not heed his own advice.

Only a peek, a flicker of unavoidable curiosity – but it was enough to discern corruption beneath the splendor.

Broken veins where a noose had tightened.

Not like them, he thought. *Whatever happens, please don't let me end up like them.*

***

Reaching the fourth floor, Declan anticipated

more ghostly theatrics.

It came in the form of throbbing orange light.

And the presence of Montha.

The light – a malevolent ochre – stemmed from a singular door at the far end.

The door throbbed and bulged.

Like something struggled to break free on the other side.

Montha, more a silhouette than anything else, appraised the newcomers.

Declan said, 'We don't have to do this. It isn't too late to retreat.'

Turning around to address something behind them, Jaison replied, 'I think you might be wrong about that.'

Declan also turned around.

To discover, smudged in shadow, a boy wearing a hood.

The kid had sprung from nowhere.

'That's not really a boy, is it?' Declan asked.

'Not anymore.'

'He's …'

'The midget I mentioned.'

Amelia's nephew.

Trying to get a fix on his face was like trying to interpret braille.

One moment, a nose presented.

Only to be swallowed up by something resembling fungus. When the suggestion of eyes appeared, they were eclipsed by bristled whiskers.

From the sleeves of a dirty, green rainslicker, rotting hands protruded.

The midget edged closer.

He's not attacking ... just herding us forward.

Comprehending the same thing, Jaison grabbed Declan's sleeve and tugged him toward the door of burning orange light.

***

Montha spoke in a voice transformed.

The voice of something infernal.

'Do you realize, caregiver, that in all the lonely years you've lived here, this is the first time you've visited me?'

Declan did not reply.

Simply studied the boy, hoping to discern some kind of chink or vulnerability.

'And you were too cowardly to come alone, I see. What do you hope to achieve by visiting me now?'

There were many reasons, of course. Conceivably, he and Jaison would discover an escape route. Or perhaps this was a prelude to a conflict that might destroy whatever abilities Montha possessed.

In the end, Declan settled for a modest riposte.

'I want to understand what's really happening here.'

Revealing luminous teeth, Montha grinned.

'You know, I was hoping you would say that. Because our hour is at hand. Everything I've been working toward … cannot be accomplished without you. Gentlemen, step into my room. Within, all will be revealed.'

***

With no time to ponder the invitation, Declan and Jaison were suddenly thrust into a bright ingress of orange light.

Propelled by what lay in front – and the dark force of the midget behind – he was swiftly separated from the writer and inserted into a dark nucleus all his own.

The orange light dissipated.

To be replaced by a concrete fortress of descending stairs.

Ushered down against his will, Declan was pushed and manhandled, the steps becoming as volatile as escalators.

Jaison had vanished.

And Declan kept descending.

An express elevator to hell …

Falling, he thought of black holes.

Of being tossed into an event horizon.

Gradually his flight slowed, and Declan apprehended hell wasn't his destination after all.

It was the central lounge of Oaklyn Castle, its

interior altered.

Have I time shifted again?

No – this was a different phenomenon.

But he *had* travelled through time.

To a period when Arabella and Boyd's renovations were still ongoing.

The lounge, containing familiar furniture, was still in a transformative state.

Portions required paint, and carpets needed pulling.

Boyd.

For some time, the man had scarcely brushed Declan's awareness.

And why would he? Boyd Palmer pulled a vanishing act right before Christmas last year – the ultimate ghost dad.

A husband and father who existed in name only.

But it was vitally important he considered him now.

Because he was seeing through the man's eyes.

Occupying his flesh.

Close by, younger versions of Kingston and Vanita were playing together on a couch – some hand game.

Next to a grand piano, a uniform-wearing Selena was explaining to her adopted father she wanted to have piano lessons once they were settled in.

'If that's okay with you,' said Selena. 'I mean, I know I was all about the saxophone last month … and I haven't entirely given up on it. But look at this piano, Dad. *Look* at it. And Mom mentioned there's two more on the third floor. It would be *criminal* not to begin lessons.'

Boyd heard his daughter.

But his attention lay elsewhere.

On the twins.

These days, his attention was *always* on the twins.

And how they were changing before his eyes.

In the beginning, these changes were small – subtle physical alterations like their eyes changing color.

Or an evil smirk from Kingston like the boy meant him harm.

Ultimately, they were things that could be attributed to Boyd's state of mind.

The stress of moving and walking through fire to adopt three children.

One evening, when Vanita began speaking in the guttural strains of a grown man, Boyd decided he wasn't suffering from stress after all.

Something was wrong with his children.

And only he seemed to be aware of it.

A short time ago – walking past their room as Declan was preparing them for bed – Boyd observed his son transforming into some kind of goblin creature.

One with reptilian eyes.

That afternoon, observing them engage in an innocent clapping game, Boyd saw the same sinister metamorphosis take place with Vanita.

All this Declan witnessed through Boyd's eyes.

A lesson concerning the past.

***

Over the months that followed, life became increasingly tense for Boyd Palmer. His new house, Oaklyn Castle, was not the utopia he'd envisaged. His wife, busy at the best of times, had progressively become consumed with expensive renovations and elaborate repairs.

Visible damage was seemingly everywhere.

From flooded wine cellars to mold-infested guest rooms.

For the first time in their relationship, Arabella's affections waned, her dedication to Oaklyn Castle superseding her desire to spend time with him.

Both had taken an extended sabbatical from filmmaking.

This did not stop Boyd's agent from mailing him a dozen different scripts in the hope he would return to Hollywood and begin shooting something family-friendly for the New Year.

But Boyd could not concentrate on film scripts.

Time and again, his thoughts strayed to the twins.

Their bizarre behavior - and change of appearance – only worsened to a point where he began to see them in an entirely new light.

Possessed by something monstrous, they were no longer his children.

Circumstances deteriorated further because of Montha, who began to show troubling behavioral signs.

Which wasn't unexpected.

The kid had been sprung from trauma; he was present at the time his real parents were slaughtered ... then subsequently transferred to an orphanage which had gone up in flames, killing dozens.

Boyd should never have acquiesced to his wife's desire to adopt.

Never.

In retrospect, he should never have given her natural children, either.

Who could have foreseen they would turn into monsters, scurrying around the mansion and biding their time to lure him into some kind of trap?

He even began to suspect Phuoc and Selena were intimate with each other.

And this was something he could not tolerate.

Not under his roof.

***

Exploring Oaklyn Castle during his downtime, Boyd soon discovered secret passageways beneath the floorboards of various rooms.

A house within a house.

Telling no one, he reconnoitered these rooms at length.

After a while, Boyd had a stunning epiphany.

Absolutely anything could happen down there.

And nobody would ever know.

Anything at all.

***

Once, Kingston and Vanita might have been children.

Now they were goblins.

The malevolent energy inside their new home had – in a process he did not comprehend – slowly seen fit to corrupt his family.

Mutating them into slavish goblin creatures who used human flesh like a suit of clothes.

***

Seducing the goblins did not prove difficult.

Possessed, there was still enough of the twins inside those little bodies to respond to adventure when it was offered.

Boyd, appealing to their curious nature, lured them into the underground labyrinth.

Once cornered against a two-way mirror, he revealed his knife.

The goblins pleaded, of course. Called him Daddy and cried. Under the guise of a false face, Vanita screamed for her mommy. When the time arrived to end them, their father never hesitated, slashing his knife through the air in a heartbeat.

Watching their tender windpipes bleed, Boyd fully expected their true forms to emerge – a goblin appendage to break through the skin in a last-ditch effort for survival.

With one body dying, a new one would be born.

But this failed to happen.

And for the first time, he wondered if they had been goblins after all.

***

Later that night, when Kingston and Vanita presented for dinner smiling and unharmed, Boyd considered the possibility he'd gone insane.

Afterward, when the vampire entered his life, the theory appeared likely.

The house.

All along, the house.

Subjecting him to individual torture.

Haunting him.

The vampire first appeared as a shadowy thing turning corners.

Then Boyd began to see him as a grinning apparition standing on stairs.

On the odd occasion, a bald head and reptilian eyes were reflected in the glass partition of doors.

A tall figure costumed in a seraphic ensemble that brought to mind Nosferatu.

From his past, Boyd knew the creature.

A distant memory all but erased.

Years ago, during his heyday acting in horror schlock, a person appeared on set donned in an old-fashioned vampire costume. At first, Boyd assumed the stranger to be of no more import than anybody else.

A man ... part of the acting scenery; someone synonymous with the present production.

Someone having every right to be there.

But Boyd's horror film was not a tale of the supernatural – did not feature creatures of the night.

And no other cast members were costumed in similar garb.

Later, he noticed the vampire's attentions were reserved solely for the star of the film.

Eerie and nonchalant, Nosferatu seemed to appear out of nowhere on any given day; his hands folded. His rheumy forehead burnished in the halogen glow of stage lighting. His eyes – also suffused with a golden shimmer – followed Boyd around with the kind of precision a birdwatcher might lavish on a rare species seldom chanced upon.

Perturbed, Boyd made enquiries among his colleagues ... and was surprised to learn no single person seemed to know what he was talking about.

They could not recall seeing a costumed vampire fitting Boyd's description.

But surely, Boyd reasoned, there was a man.

A vampire who haunted the set like some kind of demented method actor attempting to scare the creative troops.

Boyd grew frightened.

Then outright afraid.

Harboring doubts for his sanity and on the cusp of seeking help, the vampire would abruptly disappear.

Just like the celluloid vampires of old ... but lacking the puff of smoke.

Years passed.

And Boyd soon forgot about the creature.

Until he was inside Oaklyn Castle.

***

He was one of the most celebrated male actors of recent memory – but Boyd Palmer always believed there was a limit to what a man could endure.

Having to murder his children would prove to be the final straw.

Under the influence of the house, he was guilty of their demise.

And he would pay for his crime.

Yes ... Kingston and Vanita had returned.

But there could be little doubt these ephemeral versions were as fictitious as goblins.

***

On a wind-swept rainy evening, Boyd Palmer left Oaklyn Castle for the final time, escorting himself away from the property as his own judge and executioner.

Briefly, through a skein of rain, Boyd glimpsed a giant foreboding set of stairs ...

He wondered, in the aftermath of his passing, if Arabella would be okay.

Perhaps she would be.

Weeks earlier, she hatched a plan with Declan to hire a ghostwriter for her biography. For the foreseeable future, the task kept her busy. For the immediate days ahead, Boyd's preparations made it appear the movie business needed him in another part of the world – which wasn't unusual. Arabella wouldn't become suspicious of his whereabouts for weeks, possibly longer.

He hoped, ultimately, the house would not claim her.

As it had claimed the twins and Montha.

As it would soon claim himself.

***

His back to the mansion, his stride purposeful, Boyd Palmer travelled through trees and winding paths. Having seldom walked these environs, he was surprised to find himself invigorated by the experience.

Against his features, the rain felt like a sluicing away of the past.

At last, coming to Flushing Creek, he breathed a sigh of relief.

Away from the cancerous effects of Oaklyn Castle, the world here felt cleaner – the world he knew before arriving. The river, an arterial onrush of black, was silvered by the light of a hoary moon that seemed to welcome the newcomer with its own ancient indifference.

Boyd thought: Am I really going through with this?

But the thought was only half-formed when a loose tract of dirt disturbed by his arrival suddenly gave way.

With no time to right himself, Boyd plunged

downward.

In freefall, there was a brief moment to fathom what was happening.

This was his final flight from life.

Not the way he'd planned things.

But the result would be the same.

Hitting the embankment, Boyd Palmer's spine broke in two separate places.

That idolized face, adored by millions, pulverized and unrecognizable in the following days.

Perishing so far from the castle, there was little chance the Man of the Manor would return in the same manner as his children.

The house, knowing it failed to secure the father, mourned his escape.

Boyd Palmer's flesh lay on the embankment.

A mud-covered cadaver, his body concealed by the ebbing currents of Flushing Creek.

***

Passing through orange fire into a world of visions, Declan was transferred through another doorway.

A physical entrance to a factual place.

The roof of Oaklyn Castle.

Whatever authority coordinated his movement – whether Montha or house – had decided on a destination never actually broached.

The space, enormous and flat, contained a host of things.

Human beings and towering staircases.

Four separate flights, each one corresponding to a cardinal point.

Their steps hovered at the edge of the castle like airborne knolls.

At the base of the closest staircase were four human beings in the form of Arabella, two of her adopted children, and Ophelia.

Close by (in what Declan thought of as the center), Montha stood like some kind of circus showman.

The gang's all here.

Of Jaison, there was no sign.

Brought about by the sheer ambiguity of these events, Declan experienced a moment of strange vertigo.

In the leadup to tonight, he always envisioned Montha spending most of his time on the ground level, somewhere outside.

Constructing something only a transcendent species of evolution could devise.

It appeared now, his great work had been taking place up here all along.

Assembling a machine of floating staircases to usher in or out some formidable uncertainty.

Recalling the vampire's words, Declan

reflected how Oaklyn Castle had become sentient thanks to Montha.

But what did that mean, exactly?

And who is the vampire in this story, anyway?

Declan had an ominous feeling he was about to find out.

In the distance, Montha beckoned him forward with a smile.

<u>17</u>

Jaison Winters experienced a similar transition.

Twisting staircases ushered him into a wellspring of past events.

Standing in a field, he came to the slow realization he was somewhere near Oaklyn Castle.

But things were different.

This wasn't yesterday – or even months before.

Evidenced by trees uprooted during the present, Jaison had travelled into the past.

Close by, stairs shot up into the blue sky.

The same ones I stumbled across recently.

Somebody walked them.

A boy of perhaps twelve.

Nothing stood out as curious about the boy; nothing otherworldly.

His demeanor was the summation of all young boys everywhere: inquisitive, captivated.

He wore a green rainslicker and jeans.

As Jaison watched, Amelia's nephew took a few running steps forward, hesitated … then sprinted a few more.

High up, there would be dire consequences if the boy happened to fall.

But that's what I'm here to see.

More steps – and suddenly the boy was leaning down, staring over the very edge as if hypnotized.

The gardener's nephew had come across a strange object.

And decided to make it his plaything.

For a brief moment, one of the boy's shoes failed to grip.

Seconds followed as he struggled to regain balance.

Tumbling off the random stairs, Mark did not scream or cry out.

***

A long time passed before anybody noticed.

Coming across the body, Montha showed no surprise.

Only regarded Mark with something like curiosity.

Prodding the child with his toes, Montha attempted to determine if the gardener's son was dead or alive.

Blood curdling around his eyes, there was little doubt Mark was indeed dead.

Bending down, Montha grabbed one lifeless arm – began to drag the body away.

An accident, Jaison thought.

And slowly, over time, the boy returned to life.

Transformed into something monstrous.

A faceless midget with no memory of being a boy.

***

Ushered away from the mansion, Jaison's new destination was an exotic world having all the hallmarks of another country.

A place and time in Haiti when the republic, through the impetus of human evolution, would sire a gifted child.

The kind to come along once a millennium.

First, Jaison heard the sound of children in distress.

Then witnessed entire scenes as disturbing.

Children in cots, dozens of them, dirty and malnourished.

Under the gauze of stuttering fluorescents, this was an orphanage endeavoring to house more mouths than it could feed.

Among the cots, Jaison saw adult matrons, walking the rows as though they were cages. Onto a single bed, three to four babies were crammed and screaming for attention. He also saw a young boy, wise beyond his years, seeming to take on similar duties as the matrons. Big boned and water fat, the boy appeared immune to the blight afflicting others.

Montha.

Even as a youth, Jaison recognized the high forehead, dark eyes, and pointed chin.

Through shifting scenes like a film hustled at high speed, he cobbled together a story of tragedy.

Montha's mother and father, slaughtered at the hands of political dissidents. Montha, left for dead, had borne witness to the crime. Then, in the aftermath, had transported him to an illegal orphanage where hunger and discontent made headway above all else.

Calamity breeds character.

Or in Montha's case, preternatural power.

In the realm of superheroes, pain and suffering are catalysts to bring about power and strength.

Montha, subjected to barely comprehendible sorrow, underwent a similar transformation in the real world. At certain ages, he'd shown an aptitude to manipulate the minds of men.

When matrons went on to die by their own hand – those in the orphanage who partook in the physical abuse – some suspected the socially intelligent boy named Montha was responsible.

An architect pulling strings.

And Jaison realized their suspicions were correct.

For Montha had indeed mastered the art of manipulation – controlling thoughts and deeds as a puppeteer would.

Time and evolution saw these gifts evolve ... until Montha, grown into adolescence, developed the ability to make others see things that did not exist.

And there were those who caught wind of the child's power.

Seeking to thwart ambition, they desired to snuff out that power by eliminating him.

In Haiti, exhibitions of the supernatural were not uncommon.

So, it fell to certain individuals to extinguish potential messiahs before they could harness their latent abilities.

When he learned of the threats, Montha decided on his own fiery form of elimination.

By burning down the orphanage and everyone inside.

A sole survivor, Montha was transferred to another institution in the aftermath.

There he began sowing the seeds of greatness all over again.

But Montha could never have predicted the coming of something so strange and unexpected – her arrival heralded the beginning of the end.

Arabella Jaqus.

At first, Montha was confused by the woman from America.

Then outwardly curious.

The entire world was enamored with her.

And, when the wheels of adoption began to turn, he also became enamored with her – and the prospect of a new life in America.

While the move was drastic – he was forced to improve his English, in addition to sharing accommodations with other children and so much more – perhaps this was his destiny all along.

Conceivably, living in the richest country on Earth would expand his gifts and usher in a new purpose for the entire world.

How naïve Montha had been.

How fundamentally stupid!

America had not proved to be a land of opportunity.

In direct contrast, it was a vain and insipid world of consumerist greed and bankable illusions.

The biggest surprise of his relocation came in the form of the house his new mother called home.

It was no ordinary house.

A mansion with an ancient and terrible history, Oaklyn Castle used Montha as a springboard to become cognizant.

To awaken itself.

And trap everyone in the process.

***

Expelled from the past, Jaison was deposited to another location he did not recognize.

Gone were hallways and high ceilings.

Under the curtain of night, a subtle blue luminosity sheathed the strangest sight he'd encountered yet.

Staircases ascended from the roof of Oaklyn Castle.

Four of them, their flights leading nowhere.

Never visiting the rooftop before, everything present (a valley of ridge vents; a firmament of stars) told Jaison he was elevated.

Then he recalled the strange sounds from the previous afternoon outside the chapel.

From the roof, the sound of something shifting.

All along, Montha had been creating there.

In the distance, Jaison saw numerous human figures.

Then heard the first echoing rumble of thunder.

<u>18</u>

Approaching Declan and Montha, Jaison was unsure when the caregiver arrived.

But surmised he walked through his own baptism of fire – shown a bevy of past events in the lead up to this reunion.

Everything ends tonight.

Eyeing him with exhaustion, Montha said, 'Now you know, Mr. Winters. You comprehend what happened in Haiti. And you understand my mother's culpability with what's happening now.'

As in the past, the boy's words were like a trigger.

And Jaison fell into a deluge of images.

A dead kid sprawled at the bottom of random stairs, blood welling from tear ducts. Cradles lined up like cages in an orphanage filled with flies, their occupants lacking the strength to scream.

Was Declan shown similar atrocities?

'I know and understand how you set fire to an orphanage full of innocents. They were your brothers and sisters … and you watched them burn.'

'I took no pleasure in that,' said Montha. His eyes, iridescent with anger, were suddenly filled with pain. 'You saw it. Sacrifices are sometimes essential for subsistence, a greater good. My brothers and sisters were prisoners … and I went about the business of freeing them.'

'Amelia, too? Did you also free her for a greater good?'

Beside him, Declan had grown agitated. His attention, Jaison noticed, was rooted on Arabella and her children. At the base of a staircase, they were huddled together, their postures reflecting a group held captive and unable to move.

'Let them *go*,' Declan demanded. 'How is your mother responsible for any of this? How was she to know you were a freak when she decided to give you a home? How could any of us?'

'She *knew*,' Montha said, and Declan retreated back a step. 'Everybody knew, including that *witch* in her chapel. If you want to know the truth, I *am* responsible for what happened to her. You, Mr. Winters, were intimate with what she was doing. Attempting to usurp me with her imprudent and pointless magic. By the way, my sweet sister is trying a similar thing. But her mistake is thinking my abilities are tied with the arcane art of *Voodoo*. It's the American inside her, of course. When all is said and done, you fall back on superstition.'

Jaison looked at Declan. 'What did he show

you? When you went down the stairs, what kind of things did you see?'

'I saw that you were telling the truth before. Kingston and Vanita are truly dead. They were murdered by their own father.'

Jaison felt himself flounder with shock. 'Their father? What are you talking about?'

'Oaklyn Castle … it manipulated Boyd. Made him believe they were possessed. So, he killed them. Not long after, learning the truth, he killed himself.'

Having never bet Boyd Palmer outside the realm of cinema, Jaison struggled to picture the scenario. He said, 'Are you sure the house influenced him? Our friend Montha here has a talent for manipulation. Are you sure it wasn't *him* who got inside Boyd's head?'

Declan came forward again. 'He might be some kind of superhuman psychopath … but he seldom lies.'

Through the blue saturated darkness, Montha favored them with his knowing smile. 'Declan – why don't you tell Jaison what else I showed you?'

Jaison observed the caregiver shudder. 'That creature I saw inside the ballroom …'

'Wasn't human. You said it was –'

'A vampire pulled from Boyd's skull,' Montha finished. 'And given human flesh. So, Mr. Winters, your personal theory is correct. Oaklyn Castle can read the human mind and manifest personal fears. In Boyd's case, it was a long-standing terror from his past. But do you know what the vampire truly is? What lies beneath all that cloak and dagger?'

Waiting for a punchline, neither man deigned to answer.

'It's the house, of course! The *house*. Essentially, Declan's wandering Nosferatu is Oaklyn Castle incarnate.'

Again, Declan retreated.

'Do not be surprised. All this time, did you really think I was at the heart of everything? Subjecting the family to nightmares for my own pleasure? What I've been trying to tell you and what you both fail to understand, is that I'm also a casualty in this story. Before Arabella shipped me here, her trophy, Oaklyn Castle was only a mansion with a notorious history like dozens of others. Don't you *see*? I was the tinder that sparked the flames. With my arrival, I awoke the castle and gifted it sentience. In essence, I am equal parts conduit and amplifier.'

The words sounded familiar.

Then Jaison recalled hearing them during his last exchange with Montha before absconding back to the castle.

'So, this house is haunted,' he said. 'All because of you. And you blame your mother?'

Silence ensued as Montha weighed the words.

In the twilight, his teeth appeared to glow. At last, he spoke.

'We know of ghosts in Haiti … but even I was unprepared for Oaklyn Castle. When the twins returned to life as though nothing had happened to them, I fell into a deep depression. You see, the children are unaware they're dead. But their spirits are as much a part of this house as the vampire. Declan, those sounds that torment you through the walls? The sobbing? Did you not consider you're hearing the cries of the real Kingston and Vanita? That they're forever in purgatory with no means of escape?'

Judging by Declan's expression, he'd failed to consider the likelihood.

'And now,' said Montha. 'It's happened to all of us. We are all trapped in purgatory. And yet … I have discovered a means of escape.'

Revelation pinged on Jaison's awareness. 'The stairs?'

Pleased the big picture was finally bleeding through, Montha brightened.

'You're correct. The stairs are a means to escape. Do you know how long I lived in this house before discovering I couldn't leave? I will say it was time enough for Arabella to discover her own form of possession. She became, shall we say, delusional and quite insane. Thinking her children were studying in a different state, or Boyd was working in a different country. She also failed to grasp Declan's dilemma. Of course, the house had her believing the twins were still alive … they themselves fell for that ruse. Knowing I couldn't leave, I began to feel like a rat in a cage … so I began to take leisurely strolls. One afternoon, I came across a set of stairs. Random and attached to nothing, they seemed to have no function. On a whim, I decided to climb them.'

Earlier, there had been a rumbling of thunder. Now Jaison glimpsed a peel of lightning.

'That day, did I climb those stairs with the intention of ending my life? In retrospect, I think I was. Because life within this castle had become intolerable. Understand, I had tried everything to escape. I'd even attempted to open a dialogue with my captor.'

'And by captor,' Declan asked. 'You're referring to the house?'

'Yes … with the bourgeoning sentience I'd unwittingly created. But it wouldn't listen to me, of course. If the house let me walk out – then it would likely go back to being a house. Over time I began to understand the sentience was intelligent and wholly insane.'

'And you're not?' said Jaison. 'You murdered Amelia. Have a good look around you, Montha. What is the purpose of all this?'

Montha ignored the question.

'Jaison … you've seen evidence of this insanity, haven't you? The ongoing project within the house? Rooms and rooms of mannequins? What if I were to tell you those dummies are the castle's attempt to understand all it sees daily? All it *learns*. By mimicking us, Oaklyn Castle tries to comprehend humanity like some kind of artificial intelligence.'

His memories of the labyrinth still sharp, Jaison said nothing.

Walking those rooms, he recalled having a similar theory regarding their creation.

That something inhuman was endeavoring to mimic human emotion.

'But I digress. Did I mention I walked off that staircase hoping to end my existence? Well, it turned out those steps had other plans for me. There is the saying … I dipped my toes in. In this instance, that's literally what I did stepping over the edge. I dipped my toes into *another world*. Another *elsewhere*. Teetering, about to fall, I caught a glimpse of a place similar to our own – yet altogether different. I saw trees, but their leaves were like charcoal. There was sky … but the clouds were like living things. In the distance, there were houses not unlike this castle – but the bricks and windows were all fused together as though everything in this world was in the process of being devoured.

'It was only a peek, but I pulled back knowing everything had changed. Because I'd uncovered some kind of portal. For days after, I experimented, but I never crossed over. And every time I scaled those stairs, there was a foretaste of another horizon. Other dimensions teeming with wonders, but also terrors. And out of all the worlds I sampled, do you know which one I desired to enter the most? *This* world, of course. The world outside our gates. And who could have imagined that on one afternoon, my random stairs would deliver me there.'

When Montha stopped talking, Jaison returned to himself as if awakening. For his audience of two, perhaps the Haitian had induced a subtle form of hypnosis.

Or maybe the reason had simpler origins.

I've always been a storyteller. And for better or worse, I need this story to be told.

After a time, Montha resumed his tale.

'Trapped here for so long, at first, I didn't recognize where I was. Because I was *outside* the gates and looking in at Oaklyn Castle through black iron. Behind me, there was the dirt road leading away. Seeing that, my euphoria was so great I retreated again … which was a mistake.'

'You were returned to the stairs?' Declan asked.

'Yes, I was returned. And ever since that day,

I've been attempting to go back to that one elusive world.'

Declan pointed to the present stairs. 'And that's what *these* are all about? You've built your own … doorways like the one you stepped through?'

Montha smiled. It was a smile filled with admiration.

'You're a clever caregiver, Declan. Which makes me glad I've chosen you for my ritual – for our final climb. Stairways … have you ever really considered them? Stairs are the constant replication of the same structure and function. Myself … I have become a great contemplator of stairs. Think about it. Whether ancient or modern, they can be found in virtually any building. And they can also be found in perfect harmony with nature. Over eons, we've become dependent on them – much as we are dependent on the wheel. As the first simian discovered it could crack nuts with a stone, there was a first stair builder – someone who laid stone after stone to climb ever higher. And I wonder … was *that* the eureka moment for the human species? Or was it an obvious step different individuals from different civilizations happened to discover in unison? Or perhaps nature provided hints through shapes that humans tried to imitate. Symbolically, staircases suggest *journey*. They are portals uniting two things. Places, ideas … or even states of being.'

'I don't understand,' said Jaison. 'Are the stairs

a part of Oaklyn Castle?'

'No. Think of this house like space, the region beyond Earth and its atmosphere. Except space is inhabited by things like earth and stone. These four staircases, ruinous things I stumbled upon, had been placed in the cardinal points and function like black holes. Slowly, I learned they are wild cards, operated by nothing and no one. Gravity vortexes with invisible singularities. Knowing this, I brought them together where they can work as one. Soon, we will walk the flights in chorus together. And when the singularities are breached, we will be delivered out of here.'

For what felt like a long time, Jaison scrutinized Montha's entire fanciful story.

It's difficult to admit – it's a story I'm starting to believe.

Moments ago, the boy decreed lying wasn't a part of his disposition.

So, in theory, what would occur if they did as Montha asked?

Would they plummet off the edge and dash their brains out on the ground below?

Or would they step into one of Montha's described worlds and escape purgatory?

Declan, also lost in thought, decided to voice his own misgivings.

'What have you decided, Montha? That we're all going to walk off the roof because it's something that worked for you? Have you forgotten that we're human? There is nothing special about us.'

'That's where you're wrong,' Montha said. 'You imply that I am more than human – and that might be true. But so are you … and so is Arabella. How do I know this? Let us go back to staircases. In the real world, they are merely utilitarian things that facilitate ascent and descent. Not *these* staircases. These are maintained quantum shift events. In essence, they are wormholes.'

Declan said, 'Wormholes?'

Montha was nodding vigorously. 'Not only wormholes, they are symbols of power. And that's what *we* are … the four of us. Jaison and Declan, you are both scholars of the written word. And my adopted mother is a mistress of the arts. Altogether, climbing the stairs, we will be symbols of *ascension*. Of shrugging off the human taint and moving up evolution's stairs to a higher state of being.'

He's finally lost the plot, Jaison thought … and realized he suddenly felt sick.

Having travelled here originally for the purpose of writing a book, it remained incredible the dialogue with Montha could be the climax to his time in Oaklyn Castle.

And what did he learn during his stay?

That ghosts are real, and superhuman prodigies like Montha can somehow bring them into being.

Revelations had been provided.

But there was still so much Jaison remained ignorant of.

'You knew of Declan's experiences,' said Jaison. 'The sobbing in the walls, the time shifts. And you *seem* to know mine. A week ago, I saw a man from the past on the verge of suicide. Inside the chapel there was a painting on the wall, Amelia's nephew. You showed me he fell from the stairs …'

'Don't you understand? Oaklyn Castle is *conscious*. Which means it's able to construct people and events from its own layered past. It does this to pay deference to the beings who live here. Eventually, the house will resurrect you in the same manner as the twins and the *nephew*. You and Declan will be shadows in purgatory until the end of time.'

It was a depressing thought.

First, to lose your identity.

And then slowly, over time, lose corporeality.

Until you were faceless and barely formed.

A creature that stalked the living because it had no other purpose.

Jaison waved a forlorn hand toward the others. 'You said four of us would walk the flights. You said we were chosen. What about them?'

'Come with me,' Montha said.

***

'I want you to promise me something, Mr. Winters. You were summoned here to complete a task … despite what the caregiver would have you believe. And I want you to give me your word you'll complete that task.'

Montha led them to the nearest staircase. No longer at the bottom, Arabella and her family were cloistered together about halfway to the summit.

'What are you talking about?'

'The satchel you're carrying. I know you have your unfinished book inside. You brought it with you in case you *did* make it out, yes? Promise me … wherever the stairs decide to deliver you … promise me you'll tell the world. Tell the world what happened here.'

He wants the world to know he existed. Wants them to know they were denied a being that had the potential to change everything.

'You claim the castle is conscious,' Declan said. 'Why doesn't it intervene and stop what you're planning?'

'Because it's incapable of stopping me. These singularities are beyond my understanding … but they're also beyond the understanding of the house.'

As if to reinforce Montha's entire spiel, Jaison felt a burst of movement behind them.

Four figures flickered into existence.

Three child-sized people with an imposing adult in the form of a vampire.

Until now, Jaison assumed Kingston and Vanita formed a vanguard beside their mother – the huddled forms beside her. Yet here they were, small hands clutching the vampire's robe as though *he* were their mother.

The other figure was Jaison's midget, Amelia's tormented nephew.

They look like a family.

A short time ago, Montha stated the vampire was an extension of the house.

Oaklyn Castle as flesh and blood.

Now he was willing to believe it.

With an almost maternal air, the vampire placed clawed fingers upon the children's shoulders, nudged them closer.

Perhaps cognizant of their condition for the first time, the twins looked at Jaison and their caregiver with a dark longing hard to define.

Their sudden appearance was Montha's cue to react.

The motion targeting those on the staircase, he lifted one hand and flicked his wrist.

Selena, Ophelia, and Phuoc were immediately thrust backward and over the edge.

Only Arabella remained.

*****

Lightning's successor, rain began to pummel the chimneys and vent stacks.

Fused with a strain of glowing blue, the sight was evocative of impressionist art.

As if anticipating the climb, the shimmering staircases appeared expectant.

'Do not mourn Selena or Phuoc,' Montha said. 'My stepsiblings were intimate with each other. Arabella knew, of course, but said nothing.'

Trying to discern Arabella through the rain (and the bodies of her children), there was nothing to see beyond a vague blur.

Abruptly, Jaison felt a deep and profound sadness.

I was tasked with knowing her. Knowing them all. Now, I can't even say goodbye.

At the end of things, the Lady of the Manor was also a ghost.

As insubstantial as Boyd and the children.

A nobody in their story, perhaps Jaison Winters was deserving of the same fate.

***

In the blink of an eye and against his will, Jaison ascended the random stairs.

With each leg movement, he attempted to thwart the action.

And then, like the rainbow-smeared membrane of a bubble, Montha's singularity suddenly appeared.

Beyond the membrane, there were different scenes like images through an organic screen.

Jaison saw nebulae.

And rocky plains like the surface of a Jovian moon.

Burgundy like wine, there were oceans undergoing seismic shifts under the pall of titanic cyclones.

But there was also a place for the mundane – for sweeping meadows of ochre and gold.

For towering mansions whose sizes dwarfed Oaklyn Castle.

Despite the appeal of the singularity, Jaison continued to fight his ascent. At last, through sheer force of will, he twisted his head enough to glimpse the other staircases.

Near the precipice of each, a lone human figure.

Then Jaison was walking through the membrane, a final step into a world unknown.

Epilogue

Above, a noonday sun caused Jaison to blink.

By slow degrees, he moved into a sitting position.

Pressing hard against his abdomen, he could feel the leather satchel.

In tall grass, cicadas sang.

Standing upright, he discovered an equilibrium, came to understand where the final staircase had delivered him.

Gothic, bordering on medieval, Oaklyn Castle was glimpsed through the gate like something goliath, its black outline evocative of a sleeping creature with spines.

Through a scudding penumbra of overcast clouds, daylight spilled.

Besides the singing insects, there was silence.

And Jaison stood alone.

Had Arabella found her own world?

Had Declan and Montha?

What were their chances of being delivered into his sought-after realm?

Studying the roof, he saw a vague assembly of shapes.

Edifices like stairs.

Looking down at his satchel, Jaison clasped the enclosed pages with a new-found zeal.

What now? he asked himself.

Tell the world, Montha had told him.

Tell the world what happened here.

October 2021 – February 2023
Adelaide, Australia

ABOUT THE AUTHOR

A vociferous horror columnist since 2005, Matthew Tait published his first collection of dark fiction in 2011. Since then, he has won the Australian Shadows Award for his novel *Deception Pass*. Described as writing 'the sort of horror Clive Barker must read on his days off,' Matthew's fiction often treads the line between the familiar and the fantastic.